G000124790

HTML

A Step-by-Step Guide for

Beginners

GUZZLER
MEDIA

Daniel Bell

HTML& CSS: A Step-by-Step Guide For Beginners
Copyright © 2019 by Daniel Bell.

Publisher: **Amazon KDP** & **Guzzler Media LLC**

GUZZLER
M E D I A

http://www.guzzlermedia.com
Contact: contact@guzzlermedia.com
Book and Cover design by Angela W.T.
ISBN: 9781694617002
Imprint: Independently published
First Edition: April 2019

CONTENTS

Introduction

Websites are used everywhere. Every school has a website. Every church has a website. Individuals are developing personal blogs. New social media platforms are sprouting every day. Through websites, businesses are able to provide timely information to their customers. They are also able to get timely information from their customers despite their geographical location. Individuals are now able to order items and make purchases via websites. These have all been made possible by web programming languages. HTML and CSS are examples of such languages.

The good thing with HTML and CSS web programming languages is that they are easy for anyone to learn. This makes them the best programming languages for anybody who is new to computer programming. If you need to develop your own website or you are in need of becoming a professional web developer, these are the best languages to get you started. HTML will help you to create the elements that are to be added to the web page. Examples of such elements include the headers, the divisions, buttons, labels, etc. HTML will also help you to add content such as text and images to the web pages. CSS will then allow you to style and structure the elements and content in the way you want them to appear to the users. To get started with HTML and CSS, you only need a text editor and a web browser. This book is an excellent guide for you to learn web development using HTML and CSS. Enjoy reading!

1-What are HTML & CSS?

HTML stands for HyperText Markup Language. It gives content meaning and structure by defining the content like headings, paragraphs, images, etc.

CSS stands for Cascading Style Sheet. It is a presentation language developed to be used for styling the appearance of content using tools such as colors and fonts.

HTML and CSS are two independent languages and that is how they should remain. CSS code should not be written inside an HTML document ad the vice versa is true. The rule is, HTML represents contents while CSS represents the appearance of that content.

Common HTML Terms

When creating elements with HTML, you will come across

new terms. You will get used to these, but the most popular ones are elements, attributes, and tags. Let us discuss them:

Elements:

Elements are designators used for defining the structure and content of objects of a page. Some of the common elements include multiple levels of headings (from <h1> to <h6>) and paragraphs (denotes as <p> element). Other HTML elements include <a>, <div>, <strong>, <span>, <em> and many others.

To identify elements in HTML, we use the less than and greater than angle brackets < > to surround the names of the elements. Here is an example of an HTML element:

<a>

Tags:

When you use the less than and greater than angle elements to surround an element, you create a tag. Tags occur commonly in pairs of opening and closing tags.

An opening tag denotes the beginning of the element. It is made up of a less than sign, followed by the name of the element and it ends with a greater than sign. A good example of an opening tag is <div>.

A closing tag denotes the end of the element. It is made up of a less than sign, followed by a forward slash, the name of the element and lastly a greater than sign. A good example of a closing tag is </div>.

The content added between the opening and the closing tag mark the content of the element. If you need to create an anchor link, for example, it will have a starting tag of <a> and a closing tag of </a>. The content that you add in between these two tags will become the content of the anchor link. This means that you will have something like the following:

```
<a>...</a>
```

Attributes:

Attributes are properties that we used to provide additional information about an element. The most popular attributes include an *id* attribute for identifying an element, the *class* attribute for classifying an element, the *src* attribute for specifying the source for an embeddable content and *href* attribute for providing a hyperlink reference to a linked source.

We specify attributes using an opening tag after the name of the element. Generally, attributes are made up of a name and a value. The format for attributes includes the name of the attribute followed by the equals sign then the value of the attribute in quotes. Here is an example of an <a> element and a *href* attribute:

```
<a
href="http://www.facebook.com">Facebook</a>
```

The code will display Facebook on the web page and when a user clicks on it, they will be directed to https://www.facebook.com/. The anchor element has been declared using the opening <a> and closing </a> tags encompassing the text, while the hyperlink reference attribute and value have been declared in href=https://www.facebook.com/ in the opening tag.

Now that you know the meaning of the various terms, let us go ahead and explore how to come up with your own web page.

Structure of HTML Document

An HTML document is a plain text document whose name is saved with a .html extension rather than the normal .txt extension. To write your HTML code, you need a text editor that you are familiar with. However, you cannot use Microsoft Word or Pages for this as they are rich text editors. The most popular text editors for writing HTML and CSS codes are Dreamweaver and Sublime Text. Other free alternatives include Notepad++ for Windows and TextWrangler for Mac OS X.

All HTML documents are required to have a certain structure which include the declaration of the following elements: <!DOCTYPE html>, <html>, <head>, and <body>.

The <!DOCTYPE html> or document type declaration should be placed at the beginning of the HTML document and it informs the web browser of the version of HTML that is being used. Since we will use the current HTML version this should just be <!DOCTYPE html>. After the document type declaration, we have the <html> tag which denotes the beginning of the HTML document.

Inside the <html> tag, we have the <head> tag which denotes the top of the document and metadata if any (information that describes the web page). The content that you place inside the

<head> element will not be displayed on the web page itself. Instead, this may have the title of the web page shown in the title bar of the browser window, links to external files or beneficial metadata.

All the content that needs to be visible on the web page should be added within the <body> element. Here is the breakdown of the structure of a typical HTML document:

```
<!DOCTYPE html>
<html lang="en">
  <head>
    <meta charset="utf-8">
    <title>Hello World</title>
  </head>
  <body>
    <h1>Hello World</h1>
    <p>My first web page</p>
  </body>
</html>
```

The above code shows the document beginning with a document type declaration, that is, <!DOCTYPE html>, followed by the <html> element. We then have the <head> and <body> elements. The <head> element has the character encoding of the page, that is, the <meta charset="utf-8"> tag and the document's title set using the <title> element. The <body> element has the heading set using <h1> element and a paragraph set using the <p> element. Since we have nested both the heading and the paragraph within the <body> element, they will be made visible on the web page.

The code should return the following basic web page:

Hello World

My first web page

When you place an element within another element, what is known as a *nested* element, it will be good for you to keep the elements indented so as to maintain a good structure for the document.

You must have noticed that the <meta> element only has the opening tag without the closing tag. You should note that not all HTML elements have both opening and closing elements. Some elements are capable of receiving their content from attributes within a single tag only. The <meta> is an example of such an element. The contents of this element have been set using the charset attribute and value. Here are examples of other self-closing HTML elements:

-
- <hr>
- <embed>
- <img>
- <input>
- <meta>
- <param>
- <link>
- <source>
- <wbr>

The structure we have used to create our first web page is very common. Keep it as you will be using it.

Now that you are acquainted with the basics of HTML, we need to dive into CSS. Remember we stated that HTML defines the content and structure of a web page while CSS defines the visual appearance and style of the web page.

Common CSS Terms

Other than the HTML terms that we have discussed above, you should also familiarize yourself with a number of CSS terms that are very common. They include the following:

Selectors:

After adding elements to a web page, there may be a need to style them using CSS. The purpose of a *selector* is to designate the element on which we need to apply to style. The style, in this case, can be color, size or position. Selectors maybe a combination of a number of different qualifiers for selecting unique elements, and this is all determined by how unique we need to be. For example, we may be in need of selecting a certain paragraph or all paragraphs contained on a web page.

Generally, selectors target the value of an attribute, like the *id* or *class* value, or target the type of element like <p> or <h1>.

CSS selectors are followed by curly braces, { }. Inside the curly braces, we add the styles that are to be applied to the element in question. Consider the following example:

```
p { ... }
```

In the above example, we have created a select that targets all <p> elements.

Properties:

After the selection of an element, the property will determine the styles that will be applied to that element. Property names usually fall after the selector, within the curly braces, { }, and they immediately precede a colon,:.

There are many properties that we can use, as background, font-size, height, color, and width, with new properties being added on a regular basis. Consider the example given below:

```
p {
   color: ...;
   font-size: ...;
}
```

In the above example, we have defined the *color* and *font-size* properties that are to be applied to all the <p> elements.

Values:

We have used a selector to select an element to which we need to apply styles, defined the styles to apply using the *property*. The behavior of the property is determined by use of a *value*. Values are the text that is added between a colon,:, and a semicolon,;. Consider the example given below:

```
p {
   color: orange;
   font-size: 18px;
```

}

In the above example, we are selecting all the <p> elements and setting their color to orange and the size of their font to 18 pixels.

We can say that in CSS, we begin with the selector which is followed by curly braces. The property and value pairs are added within the curly braces. Each declaration begins with the property name, followed by a colon, the value of the property and then a semicolon.

You should note that CSS provides us with different types of selectors. Let us discuss these:

Type Selectors

These are the types of selectors that target elements based on their element type. A good example is when we need to target all elements of type <div>. In that case, we can use the *div* type selector. The following example shows how to create a type selector for all the division elements:

```
div { ... }
```

The above type selector will select the following HTML elements:

```
<div>...</div>
<div>...</div>
Class Selectors
```

With class attributes, we can select an element based on the class attribute value of the element. The class selectors tend to be more specific than type selectors since they select a certain group of elements instead of all the elements of a particular type.

With class selectors, we can apply the same styles to different elements at a go by use of the same *class* attribute value across many elements.

In CSS, we denote classes by use of a leading period, ., then followed by the class attribute value. Consider the following CSS example:

```
.nice { ... }
```

The above class selector will select any element that has the class attribute value, which includes both division and paragraph elements. The following HTML example shows the elements that are to be selected:

```
<div class="nice">...</div>
<p class="nice">...</p>
```

ID Selectors

The ID selectors are more specific compared to the class selectors since they only target one unique element at a time. The ID selectors use the id attribute value of the element as the selector.

Regardless of the type of the element on which they appear on, the id attribute values can be used only once for every page. If they are used, they should be reserved for specific elements.

In CSS, id selectors are denoted by a hash sign (#), followed by the id attribute value Consider the example given below:

```
#nice { ... }
```

This will select the following element:

```
<div id="nice">...</div>
```

You must have noticed that CSS selectors are very powerful. The above 3 are the most common types of CSS selectors. There are several other more advanced selectors that are provided by CSS. So what happens is that we use HTML to add elements to a web page, and then we use CSS to select those elements and apply styles to them.

Referencing CSS

For us to have our HTML file talk to the CSS file, we need to reference the CSS file within our HTML file. It is recommended that we add all our styles to a single external style sheet, then we reference it from within the <head> section of our HTML. When we use a single external style sheet, it becomes easy for us to use the same styles on an entire website and make changes quickly when necessary.

Other options that we can use to reference CSS include the use of inline and internal styles. However, these options are not recommended as when used, updating the website becomes a challenge.

To create the external CSS style sheet, we need a text editor in which we will create a file and give it a name with a .css extension. It is recommended that we save the **.css** file in the same directory or folder or within a subfolder of the .html file.

Once we have both files, that is, the .html and .css files, we can connect them by use of the <link> element within the <head> section of the .html file. Since we are linking to a CSS file, we have to use the *rel* attribute and a value of *stylesheet* to specify their relationship. We also use the *href* attribute (for hyperlink reference) to specify the location of the CSS file.

The following is an example of the head section of an HTML file that demonstrates how to set this relationship:

```
<head>
  <link rel="stylesheet" href="style.css">
</head>
```

In the above code, we are simply instructing the web browser to access the file named *style.css* and use it to apply styles to the elements of the web page. Within the *href* attribute, we have simply added the name of the file. This is because the .css file has been saved within the same folder as the .html file. If it had been saved in another folder, we could have specified the complete path to that folder. This way, the .html file will find the .css file.

Suppose the *style.css* file had been saved within a subfolder named *stylesheets*, the referencing could have been done as follows:

```
<head>
  <link rel="stylesheet"
href="stylesheets/style.css">
</head>
```

The forward slash indicates that we are moving to a subdirectory.

CSS Resets

Every web browser comes with different styles for the various elements used on web pages. The way Firefox renders headers is different from the way chrome does it. To ensure that there is cross-browser compatibility, we can use CSS resets.

The CSS resets work by picking an element and overriding the default browser styles that were to be applied to the element. This means that the same styles will be applied to the element on all web browsers. The CSS resets work by removing any sizing, paddings, margins and other styles by toning the values down.

Since CSS cascades from the top to the bottom, the reset should be added to the top of the style sheet. When you do so, the styles will be read first and the entire web browser will have a common way of rending the elements of the web page.

There are many different resets that we can use for this, with each coming with their own fortes.

2-Understanding HTML

Now that you are familiar with HTML and CSS, it is time for us to dig deeper and explore the various components that make up HTML.

For us to begin building a website, we need to know the various HTML elements used for displaying different kinds of content. You need to know how the different elements are displayed on the web page and the semantic meaning of the various elements.

Divisions & Spans

Divisions or simply <div>s and <span>s are HTML components used as containers for styling purposes. However, they do not come with any semantic value or overarching meaning. Paragraphs can be seen as semantic since any content wrapped within the <p> element will be treated as a paragraph. The <div>s and <span>s have no such meaning as they are simply containers.

However, the <div> and <span> elements are very important when it comes to web development. This is because they make it possible for us to apply common styles to a container of content.

See an <div> as a block-level element that makes it possible for us to identify a large grouping of content, and it helps us to build the layout and design of a web page. However, a <span> is an inline-level element used for identifying smaller groupings of content within a block-level element.

The <div>s and <span>s are commonly used together with *class* and *id* attributes for the purpose of styling. When choosing a value for *class* or *id* attribute, we must be careful. We should choose a value that refers to the element's content, but not the appearance of the element.

A good example is when we have an <div> element with an orange color containing social media links. We will first think of giving the <div> a class value of orange. What if the background is changed to another color such as green? It will no longer make sense for us to have a class with a value of orange. It will make sense if we give the class value of social since it denotes the content of the <div> rather than the style:

```
<!-- Division -->
<div class="social">
   <p>You can find me on...</p>
   <p>Additionally, access my profile
on...</p>
</div>

<!-- Span -->
```

```
<p>It is <span class="tooltip">easy to
create</span> HTML elements</p>
```

Notice the use of exclamation points in the above HTML content. These are not elements but they are comments. Any HTML or CSS content wrapped within a comment will not be shown on the web page. Comments provide us with an effective way of making our code organized and they also act as reminders to anyone reading through the code.

Headings

These are block-level elements and there are six different rankings for these, from <h1> through <h6>. Headings make it easy for us to break up content and create a hierarchy, and they act as the key identifiers for any user reading a web page. They are also good for helping search engines to index and determine the page contents.

The page headings should be used in an order that marks how important the page content is. The main heading for a web page should be marked as <h1> and any subsequent headings should be marked using <h2>, <h3>, <h4>, <h5> and <h6>.

Consider the following code that shows how the different headings are displayed on a web page:

```
<h1>Heading 1</h1>
<h2>Heading 2</h2>
<h3>Heading 3</h3>
<h4>Heading 4</h4>
<h5>Heading 5</h5>
<h6>Heading 6</h6>
```

The code should return the following web page:

Heading 1

Heading 2

Heading 3

Heading 4

Heading 5

Heading 6

You can see that the headings are given different sizes and bold.

Paragraphs

The HTML paragraph or the <p> element helps us to add a paragraph into a web page. The web browser is capable of adding an empty space before and after a paragraph. The <p> element denotes the beginning of a paragraph while the </p> marks the end of the paragraph. Here is an example:

```
<p>My first paragraph.</p>
<p>My second paragraph.</p>
<p>My third paragraph.</p>
```

The code will return the following web page:

My first paragraph.

My second paragraph.

My third paragraph.

Each line has been printed in its own paragraph. The text has not been styled in any special way.

If you add spaces or lines within the <p> element, the web browser will remove these. The elements added within a <p> and </p> are treated as one and are put together. Let us create an example that demonstrates this:

```
<p>
This is
my first
paragraph
in HTML.
</p>
<p>
This is my second paragraph
in HTML. I have added
many spaces                    but
the web browser will ignore it.
</p>
<p>
There is no way for you to determine the
display of HTML.</p>
<p>since when windows are resized, they give
different results.
</p>
```

The code should print the following result:

This is my first paragraph in HTML.

This is my second paragraph in HTML. I have added many spaces but the web browser will ignore it.

There is no way for you to determine the display of HTML.

since when windows are resized, they give different results.

You can see from the above image that any extra lines and spaces have been removed by the web browser.

You can use <br> and <hr> tags together with the <p> tag. The <br> is used to create a line break and it can be used with the <p> element. The following example demonstrates how this can be done:

```
<!DOCTYPE html>
<html>
      <head>
      </head>
   <body>
        <h2> Using a line break with the
paragraph tag</h2>
             <p><br>The whole class loves
      <br>Willie. Html helps us create
                 <br>web elements.
                   <br>HTML is easy to learn.
             </p>
   </body>
</html>
```

This returns the following output:

Using a line break with the pragraph tag

The whole class loves
Willie. Html helps us create
web elements.
HTML is easy to learn.

We use the <hr> element to raw a horizontal line between two lines or paragraphs. Consider the example given below:

```
<!DOCTYPE html>
<html>
```

```
<head>
   </head>
<body>
   <h2> How to draw an horizontal line
between paragraphs</h2>
      <p> The HTML hr element will draw a
horizontal line between two paragraphs to
separate them.<hr> It starts a new
paragraph.
      </p>
   </body>
</html>
```

The code will return the following output:

How to draw an horizontal line between paragraphs

The HTML hr element will draw a horizontal line between two paragraphs to separate them.

It starts a new paragraph.

The line has been drawn separating the two paragraphs.

Bold Text with Strong

To make a section of text bold to put a string emphasis on it, we can use the <strong> element, which is an inline-level element. To bold text, we can use either <strong> or <b> elements. However, the two have a semantic difference and it will be good for you to understand it.

The <strong> element is used when we need to give a strong emphasis on a section of the text, making it the most popular way of making text bold. The <b> element means that we need to stylistically offset text, meaning that it is not the best choice when we need to draw the user's attention to a certain text. This means that before making a text bold, we have to gauge how significant it is then we choose the best element to use.

Consider the example given below showing the difference between these two elements:

```
<!DOCTYPE html>
<html>
 <head>
    </head>
 <body>
    <!-- Strong importance -->
<p><strong>Warning:</strong> Site uses
cookies.</p>

<!-- Stylistically offset -->
<p>This book is good for <b>HTML</b> and
<b>CSS</b>.</p>

    </body>
</html>
```

The code will return the following output:

Warning: Site uses cookies.

This book is good for **HTML** and **CSS**.

Italicize Text with Emphasis

To write text in italics and put emphasis on it, we use the <em> element, which is an inline-level element. Just as for bolding text, there are two elements that we can use to write text in italics but the two have a different semantic meaning.

We use the <em> element when we need to put a *stressed emphasis* on text, making it the most popular way of italicizing text. We can also use the <i> element, which helps us convey text in an alternative tone or voice, just the same way as if the text was placed in quotation marks. This means that we have to gauge the significance of the text in question then we choose the appropriate element.

The following code demonstrates how to italicize text in HTML:

```
<!DOCTYPE html>
<html>
 <head>
    </head>
 <body>
 <!-- Stressed emphasis -->
<p>I <em>love</em> cats!</p>
<!-- Alternative voice/tone -->
<p>The name <i>html</i> stands for
<i>HyperText Markup Language</i>.</p>
  </body>
</html>
```

The code will return the following output upon execution:

I *love* cats!

The name *html* stands for *HyperText Markup Language*.

You can see the difference in semantics.

Text Abbreviation

To abbreviate text, you need to place it within the <abbr> and </abbr> elements. Note that the abbreviation denotes the short form of a name or word. You can add the <title> element to the code with a description for the abbreviation. Consider the example given below:

```
<!DOCTYPE html>
<html>
 <head>
     <title>Text Abbreviation</title>

   </head>
 <body>

 <p>My best friend is <abbr title =
 "Abhishek">Dr.</abbr> Nicholas.</p>

 </body>
</html>
```

The code will return the following when executed:

My best friend is Dr. Nicholas.

The title Dr. is an abbreviation.

T e x t   D i r e c t i o n

To override the current direction used for text, we can use the <bdo> element, which stands for Bi-Directional Override. Consider the example given below:

```
<!DOCTYPE html>
<html>
 <head>
     <title>Text Direction</title>
     </head>

     <body>
     <p>A text moving from left to
right.</p>
     <p><bdo dir = "rtl">A text moving from
right to left.</bdo></p>
```

```
    </body>
</html>
```

In the first paragraph, we have not used the <bdo> element, hence, the text has moved in the default direction. In the second parapgram, we have used the <bdo> element and set the *dir (direction)* attribute to *rtl* for the *right to left*. The code will return the following output:

A text moving from left to right.

.tfel ot thgir morf gnivom txet A

Underlined Text

To make a section of text underlined, we use the <u> tag. The following example demonstrates this:

```
<!DOCTYPE html>
<html>

    <head>
        <title>Underlined Text</title>
    </head>

    <body>
        <p>Web development with <u>HTML</u> is
easy.</p>
    </body>

</html>
```

The word HTML has been put between the <u> and </u> tags, hence it will be underlined. The code should return the following:

Web development with <u>HTML</u> is easy.

Strike Text

A strike is a line cutting through some text. To have such a text, we use the <strike> element. For example:

```
<!DOCTYPE html>
<html>

    <head>
        <title>Strike through Text</title>
    </head>

    <body>
        <p>Web development with <strike>HTML</strike>
is easy.</p>
    </body>
</html>
```

The text HTML has been placed between <strike> and </strike> elements, hence, it should have a strikethrough as shown below:

Web development with ~~HTML~~ is easy.

Monospaced Font

Most fonts are referred to as *variable-width* fonts meaning that different letters have different widths. For example, the letter "i" has a different width from the letter "n". The latter is wider than the former. In a monospaced font, all the letters are written in the same width. To create such a font, we place the text within the <tt> and /tt> elements. Consider the following example:

```
<!DOCTYPE html>
<html>
```

```
    <head>
        <title>Monospaced Font</title>
    </head>

    <body>
        <p>This is a <tt>monospaced</tt>
font.</p>
    </body>
</html>
```

The word "monospaced" has been placed within the <tt> and </tt> elements, hence, it should be written in a monospaced font. This is shown in the following output:

This is a monospaced font.

Superscript Text

A superscript is a text that is written above the height of the other surrounding characters. To create such a text in HTML, use the <sup> tag. For example:

```
<!DOCTYPE html>
<html>
    <head>
        <title>Superscript Text</title>
    </head>

    <body>
        <p>The is a <sup>superscript</sup>
typeface.</p>
    </body>
</html>
```

The text *superscript* has been placed within the <sup> and

</sup> elements hence it will be written as a superscript as shown below:

The is a ^{superscript} typeface.

Subscript Text

This is the opposite of the superscript text. The text is written below the height of the other characters surrounding it. To create such text, we use the <sub> element. Here is an example:

```
<!DOCTYPE html>
<html>
    <head>
        <title>Subcript Text</title>
    </head>

    <body>
        <p>The is a <sub>subscript</sub>
typeface.</p>
    </body>
</html>
```

The text *subscript* has been placed within the _{and} elements, hence, it should be written as a subscript as shown below:

The is a _{subscript} typeface.

3-Building Web Page Structure

The structure of a web page has been built using divisions for a long time. However, divisions have a problem in that they don't provide a semantic value, making it difficult to tell the intention of a division. However, HTML5 introduced new elements which are structurally based. These elements include <header>, <nav>, <article>, <section>,

<aside>, and <footer>.

The purpose of these elements is to give meaning to the way web pages are organized and improve the structural semantics. All of these are block-level elements and have no implied style or position. All of these elements can also be used severally in a web page provided each element has a proper reflection of its semantic meaning. Let us discuss this one by one.

Header

Just as the name suggests, the <header> elements help us to identify the top of a web page, section or article, or any other segment of a web page. The <header> element may have a heading, an introductory text, and navigation. It is created as follows:

```
<header>...</header>
```

Don't confuse the <header> element with the <head> element or headings <h1> through <h6>. They all have different semantic meanings.

The <header> is a structural element that identifies the heading of a page segment. It should be added within the <body> element.

The <head> element isn't shown on a web page as it only provides the metadata for a web page. Examples of such metadata include the title of the web page and links to any external files. It should be added directly to the <html> element.

The headings <h1> through <h6> help us to designate the multiple levels of text headings throughout a web page.

Navigation

The <nav> element is used for identifying a section of the major navigational links on a web page. The <nav> element should be used for primary navigation sections only, like a table of contents, global navigation, previous/next links and other groups of navigational links. It is created as follows:

```
<nav>...</nav>
```

Article

We use the <article> element to identify a section of independent and self-contained content that can be used or distributed independently. Use the <article> element to mark up newspaper articles, blog articles, user-submitted content, and other related content.

Before using the <article> element, you have to ask yourself whether it is possible for you to replicate the content elsewhere without introducing confusion. If you remove the contents of the <article> element and you place them somewhere else like in an email, they should be able to make sense. It is created as follows:

```
<article>...</article>
```

Section

The <section> element is used for identifying a thematic grouping of content, which generally includes a heading. The way of grouping content within the <section> element can be generally, but it will be good to ensure that the content is related.

Use the <section> element to break up and create a hierarchy within your web page. It is created as follows:

```
<section>...</section>
```

It may sometimes be difficult for you to determine the element to use based on the semantic meaning of the element. The trick is simple, consider the content.

The <section> and <article> elements play a significant contribution to the structure of a document and help in outlining documents. If the purpose of grouping the content is for styling purposes without adding value to the document structure, use the <div> element.

If the content has an impact on the outline of the document

and can be redistributed independently, use the <article> element.

If the content has an impact on the document outline and is a representation of a thematic group of content, use <section> element.

A s i d e

Use the <aside> element to hold contents such as inserts, sidebars and brief explanations that are related to the content surrounding it. When it is used with an <article> element, the <aside> element may be good for identifying the author of the article.

See the <aside> element as the element that is displayed off to the right or left side of a page. Remember that all structural elements including the <aside> are block-level elements and they will appear in a new line, and they will occupy the entire width provided by the web page or cover the whole length of the element they are nested within the parent element.

It is created as follows:

```
<aside>...</aside>
```

F o o t e r

The f<footer> element is used to identify the end or closing of a page, or any other segment of a web page. It is normally added to the bottom of its parent. It is created as follows:

```
<footer>...</footer>
```

Practice

We need to put all the above into practice by creating a basic website. We will use hyperlinks to link together the various pages of the website.

Step 1) We will first link the "My Website" text inside an <h1> element within the <header> element to the *index.html* page. This is the page that is first loaded when the user opens the website, showing the home page. This means that when a user clicks *My Website* text, they will be taken to the home page of the website.

This is shown below:

```
<h1>
  <a href="index.html">My Website</a>
</h1>
```

Step 2) For us to be able to navigate through the different web pages, we will create the navigation menu using the <nav> element within the header element. This will be done within the <header> element. We will add the About Us, Services, Location and Contact Us pages to go together with the Home page. We have to create links for all of these. The navigation menu can be created as follows:

```
<header>
  . . .
  <nav>
    <a href="index.html">Home</a>
    <a href="about.html">About Us</a>
    <a href="services.html">Services</a>
    <a href="location.html">Location</a>
    <a href="contact.html">Contact Us</a>
  </nav>
```

```
</header>
```

Step 3) For convenience purposes, let us add the same navigation to the footer section of the website. This can be done as follows:

```
<footer>

   . . .

   <nav>
     <a href="index.html">Home</a>
     <a href="about.html">About Us</a>
     <a href="services.html">Services</a>
     <a href="location.html">Location</a>
     <a href="contact.html">Contact Us</a>
   </nav>

</footer>
```

Step 4) In the <section> element, that introduces our website, we need to add a link that will urge them to contact us now. It will be good for this link to be added below a paragraph:

```
<section>
   . . .
   <a href="contact.html">Contact us Now</a>
</section>
```

Step 5) We need to add links to all sections that tease the other pages. Inside every section, we will wrap both <h3> and <h5> elements within an anchor element that links to the right page. This should be done for every section:

```
<section>

  <section>
   <a href="services.html">
     <h5>Services</h5>
     <h3>World-Class Services</h3>
   </a>
   <p>We served different customers from
all over the world, and these are ready to
share their testimonies.</p>
  </section>


  . . .


</section>
```

After that, you should create the other pages and make sure that they are stored in the same folder as the *index.html* file. These pages are the about.html, services.html, location.html and contact.html.

For the purpose of ensuring that all pages look the same, use the same document structure for all pages and use the <header> and <footer> elements as the file *index.html*.

Your combined code should be as follows:

```
<!DOCTYPE html>
<html>

  <header>
<h1>
  <a href="index.html">My Website </a>
</h1>

  <nav>
    <a href="index.html">Home</a>
```

```
      <a href="about.html">About Us</a>
      <a href="services.html">Services</a>
      <a href="location.html">Location</a>
      <a href="contact.html">Contact Us</a>
   </nav>


   </header>

   <body>
      <section>


   <section>
     <a href="services.html">
      <h5>Services</h5>
      <h3>World-Class Services</h3>
     </a>
      <p>We served different customers from
all over the world, and these are ready to
share their testimonies.</p>


   ...

</section>

   <a href="contact.html">Contact us Now</a>
</section>


   </body>

<footer>


   <nav>
     <a href="index.html">Home</a>
     <a href="about.html">About Us</a>
     <a href="services.html">Services</a>
```

```
      <a href="location.html">Location</a>
      <a href="contact.html">Contact Us</a>
   </nav>

</footer>

</html>
```

It should return the following:

My Website

Home About Us Services Location Contact Us

Services

World-Class Services

We served different customers from all over the world, and these are ready to share their testimonies.

...
Contact us Now
Home About Us Services Location Contact Us

4-Understanding CSS

CSS is a complex and powerful language. It makes it possible for us to lay out our pages in the way we want. We can also share such styles from page to page and from element to element. Before we can see the power of html, we need to explore some of its features for you to understand them better.

You should first understand how the styles are rendered. You need how the different selectors work and how the order of the various selectors may affect how the styles are displayed.

Cascade

To know how styles are rendered, we will study the cascade and see it in action.

In CSS, all the styles usually cascade from the top of the style sheet to the bottom, and this allows different styles to be added or overwritten with the progress of the style sheet.

A good example is when we select all paragraphs at the top of our style sheet then we set their background color to *orange*. We also set the size of the font to 22 pixels. At the bottom of the style sheet, we again select all the paragraphs and set their background color to yellow. This is demonstrated below:

```
p {
```

```
  background: orange;
  font-size: 22px;
}
p {
  background: yellow;
}
```

The paragraph selector for setting the color to yellow comes after the paragraph selector for setting the color to orange. That is why it will take precedence in the cascade. This means that all the paragraphs will have a background color of yellow. The size of the font will not change since we have not specified a new value for these in the second paragraph selector.

Cascading Properties

The cascade can still work with properties inside the individual selectors. A good example is when we select all the paragraph elements and set their color to orange, then directly below this, we set the color to yellow. This is demonstrated below:

```
p {
  background: orange;
  background: yellow;
}
```

Since the yellow color comes after the orange color, it will overrule the orange color. This means that the paragraphs will be displayed with a yellow color.

This means that all styles cascade from the top of the style sheet to the bottom. However, in some cases, the cascade does not play so nice. This is the case when different selector types are used and the specificity of the selectors breaks the cascade.

Consider the example given below:

First, let us define a paragraph with an id attribute:

```
<p id="drink">...</p>
```

The id is *drink*. Now, let us define a selector that selects paragraphs and applies color:

```
#drink {
  background: yellow;
}
p {
  background: orange;
}
```

In the above CSS, we have used two different types of selectors to select the above paragraph. The first one is an id selector while the second one is a type selector. It is true that the type selector comes after the id selector, but the id selector will take precedence over the type selector since it has a higher specificity weight. This means that the background will be shown in a yellow background.

Combining Selectors

So far, you know how to use the various selectors individually, but it is possible for us to combine different selectors. When selectors are combined, it becomes easy for us to tell the element or the group of elements that are to be selected.

Consider the HTML code given below:

```
<div class="animal">
  <p>...</p>
  <p>...</p>
  <p class="cow">...</p>
</div>
```

Our goal is to select all the paragraph elements residing within an element with a class attribute value of *animal* then set the background color to green. However, if there happens to be a paragraph with a class attributes value of *cow,* we will set its background color to brown. The CSS code for this is given below:

```
. animal p {
  background: green;
}
.animal p.cow {
  background: brown;
}
```

After a combination of selectors, they should be read from right to left.

5-The Box Model

At this point, you are familiar with the basics of both HTML and CSS. We now need to get deeper into these to know how elements are displayed on web pages and how the sizing of the elements is done.

The box model will be discussed and you will know how it works in both HTML and CSS.

Before we get deeper, it will be good for you to know the difference between block-level and inline-level elements. Block-level elements are the elements that occupy any available width, regardless of the content that they are holding, and they always begin in a new line. On the other hand, inline-level elements only cover the width that is required by their content, and they line up on the same line, one after the other. The block-level elements are used for larger contents like headings and structural elements. The inline-level elements are used for holding smaller pieces of content like a number of words selected to be made italicized or bold.

Display

The *display* property determines how the elements are displayed, whether as block-level elements, inline-level elements or any other property. Every element comes with a default *display* property value, but just like the other properties, it is possible for us to overwrite that value. There are a number of options that we can use as values for the *display* property, with the most common ones being block, inline-block, inline, and none.

To change the display property value for an element, we have to select that element within CSS then set the new value using the *display* property. If we use a value of the *block*, the element will become a block-level element. The following example demonstrates this:

```
p {
  display: block;
}
```

If we use a value of *inline*, the element will become an inline-level element. This is demonstrated below:

```
p {
  display: inline;
}
```

We can also use the value of *inline-block*. This will make the element to behave like a block-level element by accepting all the box model properties. The element will be rendered inline with the other elements, and by default, it won't begin on a new line. This can be set as demonstrated below:

```
p {
  display: inline-block;
}
```

When you use a value of *none*, the element will be hidden and the page will be displayed as if the element does not exist. The elements that are nested within the element will also be hidden. We can set it as follows:

```
div {
  display: none;
}
```

It is of great importance for you to know how the elements are displayed and how to change the value of the *display* property. The reason is that the display of an element has an impact on the way the box model is rendered.

What is Box Model?

In the box, every element on the web page is a rectangular box and it can have width, height, borders, padding, and margins. Every element is a rectangular box, and there are numerous properties that determine the size of the box. The box is defined by the width and the height of the element, which rely on the *display* property, the contents of the element, or the width and height values that have been specified. The *padding* and *border* then expand the dimensions of the box outward from the width and the height of the element. The specified *margin* will then follow the *border*.

For every part of the rectangular box, there is a corresponding CSS property, that is, height, width, border, padding, and margin. The following example demonstrates how to set the values of these properties:

```
div {
  border: 6px solid #949599;
  height: 100px;
```

```
  margin: 20px;
  padding: 20px;
  width: 400px;
}
```

In the box model, we use the following formula to calculate the width of an element:

```
margin-right + border-right + padding-right
+ width + padding-left + border-left +
margin-left
```

The height of an element in the box model can be calculated using the following formula:

```
margin-top + border-top + padding-top +
height + padding-bottom + border-bottom +
margin-bottom
```

Let us try to use the above formulas to calculate the total width as well as the total height of the element:

```
Width: 492px = 20px + 6px + 20px + 400px +
20px + 6px + 20px
Height: 192px = 20px + 6px + 20px + 100px +
20px + 6px + 20px
```

The above properties may not make sense for now. We need to take a closer look at them:

Width & Height

Each element comes with a default width and height. Even when the width and the height are 0px, the browser will by default render the element with a size. The default values for the width and height may be adequate depending on the way the element is displayed.

The default width for an element is determined by its display value. The block-level elements are assigned a default width of 100%, meaning that they consume the whole horizontal space that is available. The inline and inline-block level elements will contract to accommodate their content.

The inline-level elements don't have a fixed size, meaning that the width and height properties are only relevant to the non-inline elements. You can use the *width* property to set the width of a non-inline element as demonstrated below:

```
div {
    width: 400px;
}
```

The default height of an element depends on the content. Elements can expand vertically so as to accommodate their contents. To set the height of a non-inline element, you can use the *height* property as shown below:

```
div {
    height: 100px;
}
```

Margin & Padding

Web browsers may apply default values for margin and padding to make it clear. Text-based elements are a good example.

The default margins and paddings for such elements may be different in different browsers. These may also vary from element to element.

The purpose of the *margin* property is to help us set the amount of space that surrounds an element. The margins for elements falls outside any border and are transparent in color. We can use margins to place elements in a certain place within a web page and separate the elements. We can use it as demonstrated below:

```
div {
    margin: 20px;
}
```

The *padding* property is similar to the *margin* property but it falls inside the border of an element if the element has a border. We use the *padding* property to provide spacing inside the element. The following code demonstrates how to set the value of this property:

```
div {
    padding: 20px;
}
```

This property works on the inline-level elements vertically.

Note that you can be specific when setting the margin and padding values. For example:

```
div {
    margin-top: 10px;
    padding-left: 6px;
}
```

You are setting the margin and padding values for the different parts of the box.

Borders

The borders fall between margin and padding, giving an outline around an element. The border property takes three values, *width, style* and *color.* The values for these properties are stated in that order and in shorthand. In long-hand, these values can be broken down into border-width, border-style, and border-color properties. The longhand properties are very useful when it comes to overwriting or changing a single border value. Here is an example:

```
div {
  border: 6px solid #949599;
}
```

It is also possible for us to add borders to particular sides. This can be done using properties such as border-top, border-right, border-bottom, and border-left. This is demonstrated in the following example:

```
div {
  border-bottom: 6px solid #949599;
}
```

This can get even finer as demonstrated below:

```
div {
  border-bottom-width: 12px;
```

```
}
```

We can use the *border-radius* properties to make the corners of an element round. For example:

```
div {
  border-radius: 5px;
}
```

Box Sizing

So far, we have been using an additive design for the box model. To get the actual full width of an element, we have to add together the width, padding and border values.

We can, however, change the box model to support various calculations. The *box-sizing* property was introduced in CSS3 which can be used to change the way the box works and the calculation of the size of the elements. This property can only accept three values including content-box, padding-box, and border-box. Each of these has a different way through which the box is styled.

The default value for the property is *content-box*, which makes the box to use an additive design. If the box-sizing property is not used, this becomes the default value for the elements. The size of an element begins with the width and height, then other properties like margin, border and padding follow. Consider the following example:

```
div {
```

```
    -webkit-box-sizing: content-box;
      -moz-box-sizing: content-box;
           box-sizing: content-box;
}
```

The *padding-box* is another possible value for the box-sizing property. It changes the box model by adding any padding property values within the width and the height of the element. It can be used as shown below:

```
div {
  box-sizing: padding-box;
}
```

The *border-box* is another possible value for the *box-sizing* property. It changes the box model such that any padding or border values are included in the width and the height of the element. It can be set as follows:

```
div {
  box-sizing: border-box;
}
```

P r a c t i c e

We now need to use these styles on the web site we created in chapter 3, that is, My Website. Let's do the following:

Step 1) We need to first adjust the size of our box to make use of the *border-box* style of the box model. This will make it easy for us to resize all the elements. Create the *main.css* file and first add the following code:

```
/*
  Grid
*/


*,
*:before,
*:after {
  -webkit-box-sizing: border-box;
     -moz-box-sizing: border-box;
          box-sizing: border-box;
}
```

The * is a universal selector and it helps us to select any imaginable element and change the box-sizing property to make use of the *border-box* value.

Step 2) we now need to create a class and use it as the container for our elements. With this container, it will be possible for us to set a common width, height and other properties for all the elements that it encloses.

We will create a class with a selector of the *container* then we set the details for the container. This is shown below:

```
.container {
  margin: 0 auto;
  padding-left: 30px;
  padding-right: 30px;
  width: 960px;
}
```

Step 3) Since we have created a container class, we need to apply the class of the container throughout the HTML to both the <header> and <footer> elements of our *index.html* file. We can do this as follows:

```
<header class="container">...</header>
```

```
<footer class="container">...</footer>
```

Step 4) We need to place all the page contents at the center. We should add the container class to every <section> element within the *index.html* file. They should be changed to the following:

```
<section class="container">...</section>
```

We can now wrap the <h1> element with the <section> element with a class container. This is demonstrated below:

```
<section class="container">
  <h1>...</h1>
</section>
```

We will adjust the elements and the class later.

Step 5) Our contents are now centered. We should create a space running vertically between the elements. We need to create a bottom margin of 22 pixels as shown below:

```
h1, h3, h4, h5, p {
  margin-bottom: 22px;
}
```

Step 6) We now need to create a corner and rounded corners. Let us first add a button at the top section of the home page and below the header. This is demonstrated below:

```
<a class="btn btn-alt">Contact us Now</a>
```

We can now move to our CSS and add some styles to our classes. We should first create a new section for the buttons. We only have to create a *btn* class and specify the styles that we need to apply to all our buttons. This is demonstrated below:

```css
.btn {
  border-radius: 5px;
  display: inline-block;
  margin: 0;
}
```

Let us now add styles that will be specific to this button. We will add these using the *btn-alt* class. The following code demonstrates this:

```css
.btn-alt {
  border: 1px solid #dfe2e5;
  padding: 10px 30px;
}
```

When we use both the *btn* and *btn-alt* classes on one <a> element, we allow the styles to be layered on, and all styles will be rendered on a single element.

Step 7) We also need to add some padding to the <section> element that has the <a> element with the *btn* and *btn-alt* classes. We will add some class attribute value *hero* to the <section> element, together with the *container* class attribute value, as it will make the leading page for the website:

```html
<section class="hero container">
  ...
</section>
```

We can then create a new section within the CSS file for the home page styles.

```
.hero {
  padding: 22px 80px 66px 80px;
}
```

You must make sure that you have linked your *main.css* file to the *index.html* file. If not, you only have to add the following line within the header section of the .html file:

```
<link rel="stylesheet" href="main.css">
```

At this point, your *index.html* file should have the following code:

```
<!DOCTYPE html>
<html>

<header>
<link rel="stylesheet" href="main.css">
<h1>
  <a href="index.html">My Website </a>
</h1>

  <nav>
    <a href="index.html">Home</a>
    <a href="about.html">About Us</a>
    <a href="services.html">Services</a>
    <a href="location.html">Location</a>
    <a href="contact.html">Contact Us</a>
  </nav>


  </header>

<section class="hero container">
<a class="btn btn-alt">Contact us Now</a>
</section>
```

```
    <body>
      <section class="container">
  <section>
    <a href="services.html">
      <h5>Services</h5>
      <h3>World-Class Services</h3>
    </a>
    <p>We served different customers from
all over the world, and these are ready to
share their testimonies.</p>



  ...


</section>

</section>


    </body>

<footer>


  <nav>
    <a href="index.html">Home</a>
    <a href="about.html">About Us</a>
    <a href="services.html">Services</a>
    <a href="location.html">Location</a>
    <a href="contact.html">Contact Us</a>
  </nav>


</footer>

</html>
```

The *main.css* file should have the following code:

```
/*
```

```
   Grid
*/


*,
*:before,
*:after {
  -webkit-box-sizing: border-box;
     -moz-box-sizing: border-box;
          box-sizing: border-box;
}


.container {
  margin: 0 auto;
  padding-left: 30px;
  padding-right: 30px;
  width: 960px;
}


h1, h3, h4, h5, p {
  margin-bottom: 22px;
}




.btn {
  border-radius: 5px;
  display: inline-block;
  margin: 0;
}


.btn-alt {
  border: 1px solid #dfe2e5;
  padding: 10px 30px;
}
```

```css
.hero {
  padding: 22px 80px 66px 80px;
}
```

6-Positioning Content

With CSS, it is possible for us to position our content and elements in almost any imaginable way, meaning that we can have a structure that well suits our design and have content that is more digestible.

There are different types of positioning used in CSS, and each has its own application. We will discuss some of these in this chapter:

Floats

A *float* is one of the best ways for us to position an element on a web page. It is a versatile property and we can use it in a number of different ways.

With the float property, we take an element, separate it from the normal flow of the web page, then we position it to the right or left of its parent element. The other page elements will then flow around the floated element. The most popular values for the *float* property are *right* and *left* and they can be set as shown below:

```
img {
    float: left;
}
```

Practice

We want to see floats work. We will create a basic page layout having a header at the top, two columns at the center and a footer at the bottom. The page will be marked using the <header>, <section>, <aside> and <footer> elements.

Create both the *.html* and the *.css* files. You can name the .html file as *index.html* while the .css file as *style.css*.

Add the following code to the *index.html* file:

```
<html>
<header>
<link rel="stylesheet" href="style.css">
  <code>&#60;Header&#62;</code>
</header>

<section>
  <code>&#60;Section&#62;</code>
</section>

<aside>
  <code>&#60;Aside&#62;</code>
</aside>

<footer>
  <code>&#60;Footer&#62;</code>
```

```
</footer>
</Html
 >
```

Notice the use of the <code> element. It stands for computer code, so it will be interpreted as such. We are using it to style the text that we need to appear on the web page. See the following line for example extracted from the above code:

```
<code>&#60;Header&#62;</code>
```

We have just used the <code> element to style how the *Header* text will be printed on the web page.

Notice that we have linked the .html file to the .css file in the header.

The <section> and <aside> elements are block-level elements, hence, they will be stacked on top of each other by default. However, our goal is to see them displayed side by side. If we float the <section> element to the left and the <aside> element to the right, they will be rendered as two columns sitting opposite of each other. To make this happen, we can create the following CSS:

```
code {
  background: #2db34a;
  border-radius: 6px;
  color: #ecf;
  display: block;
  font: 14px/24px Inconsolata, "Lucida
Console", Terminal, "Courier New", Courier;
  padding: 24px 15px;
  text-align: center;
}
header,
section,
```

```
aside,
footer {
  margin: 0 1.5% 24px 1.5%;
}
footer {
  margin-bottom: 0;
}
```

The codes should return the following web page:

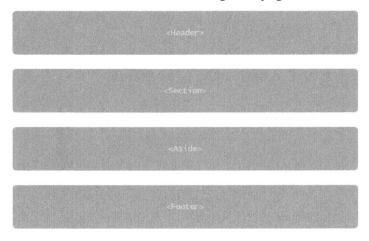

Note that by default, when an element is floated, it will be moved to the edge of its parent element. If there is no parent element, the element will float to the end of the web page. However, this is not what we need. We need to shape the web page structure so that it may be nice. This means we use *margin* and *width* properties to the *style.css* file as shown below:

```
code {
  background: #2db34a;
  border-radius: 6px;
  color: #ecf;
  display: block;
  font: 14px/24px Inconsolata, "Lucida
Console", Terminal, "Courier New", Courier;
  padding: 24px 15px;
  text-align: center;
}
```

```
header,
section,
aside,
footer {
  margin: 0 1.5% 24px 1.5%;
}
section {
  float: left;
  width: 63%;
}
aside {
  float: right;
  width: 30%;
}
footer {
  clear: both;
  margin-bottom: 0;
}
```

When you re-run the code, you will notice a change in the <Section> and <Aside> elements. They will be placed side-by-side as shown below:

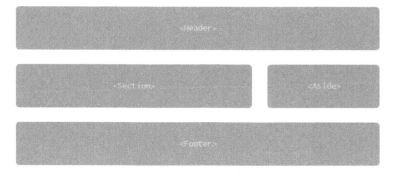

For the case of two columns, we only have to float one to the left and the other one to the right. However, when dealing with three columns, we have to change the approach. Suppose we need to use three columns between the <header> and <footer> elements. We can drop the <aside> element and instead use <section>

elements as shown below:

```html
< html>
<header>
<link rel="stylesheet" href="style.css">
  <code>&#60;Header&#62;</code>
</header>

<section>
  <code>&#60;section&#62; </code>
</section>

<section>
  <code>&#60;section&#62; </code>
</section>

<section>
  <code>&#60;section&#62;</code>
</section>

<footer>
  <code>&#60;footer&#62;</code>
</footer>
</Html>
```

Notice the three <section>…</section> elements between the <header> and <footer> sections.

Our goal is to have these three <section> elements placed in a three-column row. For the case of two columns, we floated one to the left and the other to the right. For three, we will float all of them to the left. Since we have added another <section> element, we have to adjust their widths so as to fit in the row. This means that we should modify the section selector to the following CSS:

```css
section {
  float: left;
  margin: 0 1.5%;
  width: 30%;
```

```
}
```
You should now have the following CSS:
```
code {
  background: #2db34a;
  border-radius: 6px;
  color: #ecf;
  display: block;
  font: 14px/24px Inconsolata, "Lucida
Console", Terminal, "Courier New", Courier;
  padding: 24px 15px;
  text-align: center;
}
header,
section,
aside,
footer {
  margin: 0 1.5% 24px 1.5%;
}
section {
  float: left;
  width: 30%;
}
footer {
  clear: both;
  margin-bottom: 0;
}
```

These should generate the following web page:

We have three <section> columns and all have an equal amount of width.

Clearing Floats

The *float* was initially developed to help in allowing content to be wrapped around images. One could float an image, then have all the content surrounding the image to flow naturally around it. When the *float* property is used for layout and positioning of elements, it brings a lot of challenges.

To prevent the content from wrapping the floated elements, we have to clear or contain those floats then have the page back to its normal flow. We will first explore how to clear floats then we discuss how to contain floats.

To clear floats, we use the *clear* property. The property accepts a number of values, with the most common ones being *left, right* and *both.* It can be used as shown below:

```
div {
    clear: left;
}
```

We have set the value of clear property to *left*, meaning that it will clear all the left floats. If we use a value of the *right,* all the right floats will be cleared. The value *both* will clear both the right and the left floats.

Let us use the example where we had two columns in the middle row, the <section> and <aside> columns. We need to use the value of *both* for the clear property on the <footer> element.

You will see that both floats will be cleared. It is always advisable that the clear property should be applied to an element that appears after the floated elements, rather than before, and the page will be returned to the normal flow. We can set the property as shown below:

```
footer {
    clear: both;
}
```

This means that you should have the following CSS:

```
code {
    background: #2db34a;
    border-radius: 6px;
    color: #ecf;
    display: block;
    font: 14px/24px Inconsolata, "Lucida
Console", Terminal, "Courier New", Courier;
    padding: 24px 15px;
    text-align: center;
}
header,
section,
aside,
footer {
    margin: 0 1.5% 24px 1.5%;
}
section {
    float: left;
    width: 63%;
}
aside {
    float: right;
    width: 30%;
}
footer {
    clear: both;
    margin-bottom: 0;
}
```

See the *clear* property has been set to *both* in the footer selector. This should return the following web page:

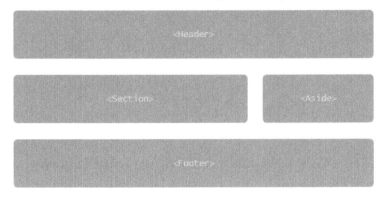

Containing Floats

We can also contain floats instead of clearing them. The two have almost similar outcomes, but containing floats will help us ensure that all the styles are rendered properly.

To contain a float, the floated element must reside within the parent element. In that case, we will have the parent element acting as the container, and the flow of the document outside the container will be left to normal. The parent element, which is represented by the *group* class will have the CSS give below:

```css
.group:before,
.group:after {
  content: "";
  display: table;
}
.group:after {
  clear: both;
}
.group {
  clear: both;
  *zoom: 1;
```

```
}
```

The above CSS is simply clearing any elements within the element that are floated with the *group* class and returning the flow of the document to a normal. You can see the: *before* and: *after* pseudo-elements which are generated dynamically above and below the elements with the *group* class. Such elements don't have any content and they are displayed in the form of table-level elements, similar to the block-level elements.

The element generated dynamically after the element with the *group* class will clear the floats within the element with the *group* class.

By use of our two-column layout page, we will wrap the <section> and the <aside> elements within a parent element. The parent element will be in need of containing the floats within itself.

Your HTML code in the *index.html* file should be as follows:

```
<Html>
<header>
<link rel="stylesheet" href="style.css">
  <code>&#60;Header&#62;</code>
</header>

<div class="group">

  <code class="default">&#60;section="group"&#62;</code>

  <section>
    <code>&#60;Section&#62; </code>
  </section>

  <aside>
    <code>&#60;Aside&#62; </code>
  </aside>
```

```
</div>

<footer>
  <code>&#60;Footer&#62; </code>
</footer>
</Html>
```

See that the <section> and <aside> elements have been wrapped within a <div> element and a *group* class. Your CSS should be as follows:

```css
code {
  background: #2db34a;
  border-radius: 6px;
  color: #ecf;
  display: block;
  font: 14px/24px Inconsolata, "Lucida
Console", Terminal, "Courier New", Courier;
  padding: 24px 15px;
  text-align: center;
}
.default {
  background: none;
  color: #666;
}
.group:before,
.group:after {
  content: "";
  display: table;
}
.group:after {
  clear: both;
}
.group {
  background: #eaeaed;
  border-radius: 6px;
  clear: both;
```

```
  *zoom: 1;
}
.group,
header,
section,
aside,
footer {
  margin: 0 1.5% 24px 1.5%;
}
section {
  float: left;
  width: 63%;
}
aside {
  float: right;
  width: 30%;
}
footer {
  margin-bottom: 0;
}
```

The codes should return the following web page:

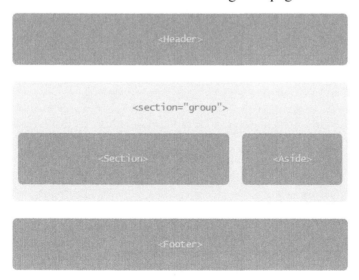

The technique for containing elements as demonstrated above is referred to as *clearfix* and can be found in websites with the name *clearfix* or *cf.* We used a class name of the *group* since it represents a group of elements and it expresses the content better.

Relative Positioning

When you set the value of the *position* property to a *relative*, the elements will be made to appear within a normal flow within a page, and space will be left for the element as intended and other elements will not be allowed to flow around it. However, it is possible for us to modify the display position of the element using the box offset properties. For example, suppose you have the following HTML:

```
<Html>
<header>
<link rel="stylesheet" href="mystyle.css">
</header>
<div>
  <code>&#60;div&#62;</code>
</div>

<div class="offset">
  <code>Offset</code>
</div>

<div>
  <code>&#60;div&#62;</code>
</div>
<Html>
```

We can apply the following CSS to the above HTML. This is

the *mystyle.css* file:

```css
code {
  color: #666;
  font: 14px/24px  Inconsolata, "Lucida
Console", Terminal, "Courier New", Courier;
}
div,
.offset code {
  border-radius: 6px;
}
div {
  background: #eaeaed;
  height: 62px;
  padding-top: 38px;
  text-align: center;
  width: 100px;
}
.offset {
  background: none;
  border: 2px dashed #9799a7;
  height: 100px;
  padding: 0;
}
.offset code {
  background: #2db34a;
  color: #fff;
  display: block;
  height: 74px;
  left: 20px;
  padding-top: 26px;
  position: relative;
  text-align: center;
  top: 20px;
  width: 100px;
}
```

These two should return the following:

In the above example, the second div element, which has the offset class has been created with a value of *relative* for the *position* property. There are also two box offset properties with values of *left* and *top*. Due to this, the original position of the element has been maintained, and the rest of the elements are not allowed to get into space. The box offset properties have also repositioned the element by pushing it by 20 pixels from the top and 20 pixels from the left from the original location.

Absolute positioning

Wan element with a value of *absolute* for the *position* property will be different from an element with a value of *relative* for the same *property*. When an element is given a value of *absolute* for this property, its positioning will not be according to the normal flow of the document. At the same time, the original position and space of the element positioned absolutely won't be preserved.

What happens is that an element that is positioned absolutely is moved in relation to its closest element positioned relatively. If there is no such a parent element, that is, one with a relative position, the element will be moved or positioned in relation to the <body> element. Let us demonstrate how this works. You should have the following HTML:

```
<Html>
<header>
<link rel="stylesheet" href="mystyle.css">
</header>
<section>

  <code> position: relative</code>

  <div class="offset">
    <code>position: absolute </code>
  </div>

</section>

<Html>
```

The .css file should have the following code:

```
code {
  color: #666;
  font: 14px/24px Inconsolata, "Lucida
Console", Terminal, "Courier New", Courier;
}
section,
.offset,
.offset code {
  border-radius: 6px;
  padding: 24px 30px;
}
section {
  background: #eaeaed;
```

```
  height: 145px;
  position: relative;
}
.offset,
.offset code {
  height: 96px;
  position: absolute;
  width: 160px;
}
.offset {
  border: 2px dashed #9799a7;
  right: 0;
  top: 0;

}
.offset code {
  background: #2db34a;
  color: #fff;
  display: block;
  right: 20px;
  top: 20px;
}
```

The code should return the following web page:

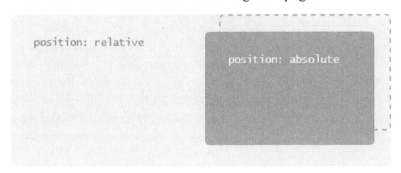

The <section> element has been positioned relatively but it has no box offset properties. Consequently, its position has not changed. The <div> element with the *offset* class has a value of *absolute* for the *position* property. Since the <section> element forms the closest parent element that is positioned relatively to the <div> element, this <div> element will have to be positioned relatively to the <section> element.

Practice

In this practice, we will be working on our website, that is, My Website. We need to add more content to the website and place it at the center of the web page. Do the following:

Previously, we changed the box-size to use *border-box* version of the box model as it makes it easier for us to size the elements.

We used the universal selector, *, together with the universal pseudo-elements, *: before and *:after, so as to select each imaginable element then change the *box-sizing* property to *border-box*.

We now have an understanding of reusable layouts, so we can implement one on our website. Follow these steps:

Step 1) We will come up with a three-column reusable layout for our website by the use of inline-block elements. Add the following lines to the grid section of the file *main.css*:

```
.col-1-3 {
  width: 33.33%;
}
.col-2-3 {
  width: 66.66%;
}
```

The above code will help us to create the columns.

Step 2) Our goal is to have the elements displayed as inline-block elements. We want to ensure that the vertical alignment is set at the top of every column too.

We can now create two other selectors for sharing the display and set the property styles for the vertical alignment. This is shown below:

```css
.col-1-3,
.col-2-3 {
  display: inline-block;
  vertical-align: top;
}
```

Above, we have created two class selectors that are separated from each other by a comma.

Step 3) space is needed between the columns so that we may have the content separated. To accomplish this, we will use horizontal padding on the columns. This will work well but space will become double as the columns sit next to each other. We need to balance this, hence, we will have our columns added within a grid then add similar padding from the columns to the grid.

We will identify the grid using a class of *grid*, then identify the same horizontal padding for the grid, the *col-1-2* and *col-2-3* classes. We will still use a command to separate our selectors, hence we should add the following CSS:

```css
.grid,
.col-1-3,
.col-2-3 {
  padding-left: 15px;
  padding-right: 15px;
}
```

Step 4) We need to share some of the styles from the *container* rule set with the *grid* rule set. This means that we will share the *width* property and values as well as the *margin* property and values. To accomplish this, we will break up the old *container* rule set to get the following:

```
.container,
.grid {
  margin: 0 auto;
  width: 960px;
}
.container {
  padding-left: 30px;
  padding-right: 30px;
}
```

With the above CSS, it means that any element that belongs to the *grid* or *container* class will have a width of 960 pixels and it will be placed at the center of the page.

Step 5) All the work that was needed to have the reusable grid styles well styles have been completed. We should now work with the HTML and see the classes in action. We will work on the home page, the index.html file. Currently, our teasers are wrapped within the <section> element and a class of *container* has been used. Let us change the class from *container* to *grid* then we begin to place the columns within it. This is demonstrated below:

```
<section class="grid">
  ...
</section>
```

Step 6) We now need to add the class *col-1-3* to all <section>

elements within the <section> element that has a *grid* class. This means it should be done as follows:

```
<section class="grid">
  <section class="col-1-3">
    . . .
  </section>
  <section class="col-1-3">
    . . .
  </section>

  <section class="col-1-3">
    . . .
  </section>

</section>
```

Step 7) Since every column is an inline-block element, we should ensure that any empty space between them is removed. We will do this by use of comments as shown below:

```
<section class="grid">

  <!--About Us -->

  <section class="col-1-3">
    . . .
  </section><!--

  Services

  --><section class="col-1-3">
    . . .
  </section><!--

  Location
```

```
--><section class="col-1-3">
  ...
</section><!--
```

Location

```
--><section class="col-1-3">
  ...
</section><!--
```

Contact us

```
--><section class="col-1-3">
  ...
</section>

</section>
```

7-Typography

With typography, it is possible for us to come up with a system of our fonts and embed them into a website.

Initially, there were only a few typefaces that we could use on websites. These were the fonts that were installed on computers, hence they were the ones with the possibility of rendering text well on the screen. If a font was not installed on a computer, it could not be rendered on a website. Since we now have the ability to embed fonts, we have a wide variety of typefaces to choose from, including the ones that we add to a website.

It is true that we can get new fonts on websites so as to get a wide variety of typefaces, but it is good for us to be aware of the principles of typography.

Typeface vs. Font

These two terms are commonly used interchangeably, but they have a different meaning.

The *typeface* is what we are allowed to see. See it as the artistic impression that determines how text feels, looks, and reads.

The *font* is the file that contains the typeface. When you use a font on a computer, the computer will be allowed to access the typeface.

Text Color

When developing a website, it is good for you to determine the typeface and the color that you will use. The typeface and color of text play a great significance in determining the legibility and look of a web page. We need to override the defaults offered by the web browser and customize the page to be the way we want it to be.

To set the text color, we use the *color* property of CSS. This property accepts the value of one color, which can be in different formats. Consider the example given below:

```
html {
  color: #555;
}
```

In the above CSS, we are changing the color of any text that appears within the <html> element on the web page.

Font Family

We use the *font-family* property to determine the font as well as the fallback or substitute fonts that are to be used for displaying text. The property takes several values which are font names, all separated by commas.

The first font declared on the left becomes the primary font choice. If the primary font is not found, the alternative fonts will be declared, with the preference running from the left to the right.

If one of the fonts has a name that is made up of more than one words, these should be enclosed within quotation marks. Also, the last font has to be a keyword value, and it will make use of the default system font for the specified type, and this is commonly the *sans-serif* or *serif*.

Consider the example given below:

```
body {
  font-family: "Helvetica Neue", Arial,
Helvetica, sans-serif;
}
```

In the above example, the preferred font for display is *Hevetica Neue*. If this font is not found, maybe because it is not installed on the device, the second one, *Arial* will be considered. This continues.

Font Size

With the *font-size* property, we can set the size to be used for text by use of the common length values such as percentages, em units, points, pixels or font-size keywords. Consider the example given below:

```
body {
  font-size: 12px;
}
```

In the above example, we are setting a size of 12 pixels for the text added within the <body> element.

Font Style

We can use the *font-style* property to write the text in italics or prevent the text from being italicized. The *font-style* property can only accept four values, that is, *normal, italic, oblique,* and *inherit.* The normal and italic are the most common values for this property.

Consider the example given below:

```
.special {
  font-style: italic;
}
```

The above CSS will set all elements with a class of *special* to print the text in italics.

Font Variant

It is always a necessity fo0r a text to be set to small capitals, also referred to as *small caps.* This can be done using the *font-variant* property. This property can accept three values only, namely *normal, small-caps,* and *inherit.* The most popular values for this property are *normal* and *small-caps* which can be used for switching typefaces between the normal and small caps variants.

Consider the following example:

```
.firm {
  font-variant: small-caps;
}
```

In the above example, we have switched all elements with the class *firm* to use small caps as the font-variant.

Font Weight

In some cases, we will need to write text in bold or change the weight of the typeface. We can do this using the *font-weight* property. This property can accept either numeric or keyword values.

The keyword values are *normal, bold, bolder, lighter, and inherit*. It is always recommended that you use *bold* and *normal* so as to change your text from normal to bold and vice versa. Instead of using the values *bolder* or *lighter* it is recommended that you use a numeric value so as to set the value of the weight.

Consider the example given below:

```
.daring {
  font-weight: bold;
}
```

In the above example, we have set the font to *bold* for any element that has the class *daring*. You can also use numeric values of 100, 200, 300, 400, 500, 600, 700, 800, and 900 for typefaces that come with multiple weights. The order, in this case, begins with the thinnest weight and ends with the thickest of all weights, that is, 100 to 900. The *normal* weight corresponds to a value of 400 while the *bold* weight corresponds to a value of 700.

A numeric value for this property can be set as follows:

```
.daring {
  font-weight: 500;
}
```

The above code sets a font weight of 500 on all elements with a *daring* class.

Line Height

Line height is the distance between two lines of text. We can set this using the *line-height* property. This property can accept values of general length.

It is recommended that you set the value of this property to one and half times the size of the *font-size* property. This means that you just set the value of this property to 150% or 1.5. However, for the case of the baseline grid, we can use pixels so as to have more control over the line-height property.

Consider the example given below:

```
body {
  line-height: 20px;
}
```

In the above example, we have set a line-height of 20 pixels for contents added within the <body> element. This means that a line-height of 20 pixels will be used within the element.

We can also use the line-height property to center a single line of text vertically within an element. We can use the properties of *height* and *line-height* so as to center the text vertically. The following example demonstrates this:

```
.btn {
  height: 20px;
  line-height: 20px;
}
```

The above is a technique very popular with alert messages, buttons, as well as other single line text blocks.

Shorthand Font Properties

All the font properties discussed above can be combined together into a single font property and a shorthand value. The *font* property is capable of accepting multiple property values based on font. Note that the order of the values will matter a lot and they should be written as follows from left to right:

```
font-style, font-variant, font-weight, font-
size, line-height, font-family
```

The values should be listed from left to right without separating them with a comma except for the case of font names since the *font-family* property has to use commas.

Use a forward slash (/) to separate the values for *font-size* and *line-height*.

When we use the shorthand value, each property value is optional other than the *font-family* and *font-size* properties. This means that it is possible for us to include only the *font-family* and *font-size* property values in shorthand value if that is what we desire to have. The following example demonstrates this:

```
html {
  font: italic small-caps bold 12px/20px
"Helvetica Neue", Helvetica, Arial, sans-
serif;
}
```

Combining Font Properties

We want to create an example that demonstrates how to use all the above font properties. Add the following code to your .html file:

```
<Html>
<header>
<link rel="stylesheet" href="mystyle.css">
</header>


<h2><a href="#">Web developer</a></h2>

<p class="byline">Posted by Alex</p>

<p> This example demonstrates how to use all
the CSS font properties <a
href="#">Continue&#8230;</a></p>

<Html>
```

We have only created a number of HTML elements to help us add text to the web page. Add the following code to your .css file, that is, *mystyle.css*:

```
h2,
p {
  color: #654;
```

```
    font: 14px/22px "Helvetica Neue",
Helvetica, Arial, sans-serif;
}
a {
    color: #0287cc;
}
a:hover {
    color: #fc7b27;
}
h2 {
    font-size: 20px;
    font-weight: bold;
    margin-bottom: 8px;
}
.byline {
    color: #6759a6;
    font-family: Georgia, Times, "Times New
Roman", serif;
    font-style: italic;
    margin-bottom: 20px;
}
```

The codes should return the following web page:

Web developer

Posted by Alex

This example demonstrates how to use all the CSS font properties Continue...

Practice

We want to get back to our website, that is, My Website, and add some font-based properties to it. Do the following:

Step 1) We should first update the font on all the text. We only have to apply the necessary styles to the <body> element. We will add properties such as color, font-weight, font-size, font-family, and line-height. We will set these using the shorthand *font* property. Let us add these just have the grid section and below the reset in the main.css file:

```css
body {
  color: #768;
  font: 300 18px/20px "Open Sans", "Helvetica Neue",
Helvetica, Arial, sans-serif;
}
```

Step 2) We had previously added some typographic styles, specifically the bottom *margin* to different levels of headings and paragraphs. Within that section in the main.css file, we will add a color to the <h1> to <h4> elements. Add the following code:

```css
h1, h2, h3, h4 {
  color: #728882;
}
```

We also need to set the font sizes for the various levels of headings. To make the text eligible, we have to set the *line-height* property. Here is the CSS code for this:

```css
h1 {
  font-size: 34px;
  line-height: 42px;
}
h2 {
  font-size: 22px;
  line-height: 42px;
}
```

```
h3 {
  font-size: 20px;
}
h4 {
  font-size: 17px;
}
```

Step 3) We want to make all our <h5> elements to be unique and different from the other elements. We will do this by modifying their styles a bit.

We will change their color and use a smaller value for the font-size property. We will also use a font-weight of normal or 400.

The default setting is that a web browser will render headings using a font-weight of bold. However, we have headings using a different font size. When we use a font-weight of 400 on all <h5> elements, they will appear thicker than the rest of the headings. The following CSS will help us achieve this:

```
h5 {
  color: #a8c2b7;
  font-size: 14px;
  font-weight: 400;
}
```

Step 4) We want to use a font-weight of 400 for all our <strong> elements, which is equal to normal rather than bold. This is because we are using a typeface that is a bit thick compared to the rest. For all the <em> and <cite> elements, we want to use a font-style of italics. We can set these as follows:

```
strong {
  font-weight: 400;
}
```

```
cite, em {
  font-style: italic;
}
```

Step 5) We now need to add some styles to the anchor elements. Currently, they are using the default settings of the web browser. We want them to use the same color as the <h1> to <h4> elements. We will also use the: hover pseudo class so as to change the color to light gray anytime the user hovers over the anchor.

```
a:hover {
  color: #a9b2b9;
}
a {
  color: #648880;
}
```

Step 6) Now, let us have a closer look at the <header> element to update its styles. Consider a logo for a website. It should be located on the top left. The following properties can help us to position and style our logo:

```
.logo {
  border-top: 4px solid #648880;
  float: left;
  font-size: 48px;
  line-height: 44px;
  padding: 40px 0 22px 0;
}
```

Step 7) Since the size of the logo has been bumped, we should add a margin to our <h3> element within the <header> so that it may stay balanced. We will add a class of *tagline* to the <h3> element then we use the *.tagline* selector to apply the margins within our CSS file.

Here is the <h3>:

```
<h3 class="tagline">Welcome to My Website.
Enjoy our services</h3>
```

Here is the CSS for the above:

Step 8) After the <h3> element, we have the <nav> element. We want to add to it the primary-nav class attribute then we set the *font-weight* and *font-size* properties. This will make the navigation to stand out against the rest of the header elements. Here is the html code for this:

```
<nav class="primary-nav">
    <a href="index.html">Home</a>
    <a href="about.html">About Us</a>
    <a href="services.html">Services</a>
    <a href="location.html">Location</a>
    <a href="contact.html">Contact Us</a>
</nav>
```

Here is the corresponding CSS for the <nav>. Add it to your main.css file:

```
.primary-nav {
  font-size: 14px;
  font-weight: 400;
}
```

Step 9) We now have the <header> element looking a bit

better. We now need to have a look at the <footer> element. We will add the *primary-footer* class to the element, then we use a selector in our CSS file to change the color and font-size for the text added to the footer. We will also set the font-weight of the element <small> to 400 as shown below:

```
.primary-footer {
  color: #758890;
  font-size: 14px;
  padding-bottom: 44px;
  padding-top: 44px;
}
.primary-footer small {
  float: left;
  font-weight: 400;
}
```

Step 10) We now need to make some updates to the home page. We will begin with the hero section and increase its line-height to 44 pixels. We will also enlarge the text within this section, and increase the size of <h2> element to 36 pixels. For the <p> element, we will use a font size of 24 pixels.

The changes will be made by use of the current hero selector within our CSS file. We will then create new selectors for the <h2> and <p> elements. The styles for the hero section should now be as follows:

```
.hero {
  line-height: 44px;
  padding: 22px 80px 66px 80px;
}
.hero h2 {
  font-size: 36px;
}
```

```
.hero p {
  font-size: 24px;
}
```

Step 11) We lastly need to fix a small issue on our web page. We added a light gray color to the anchor elements after the user hovers over them. This should work well except for where we have three teasers within the home page with the anchor element wrapping both <h3> and <h5> elements. This is because the elements have their own color definition and the: *hover* pseudo-class styles doesn't affect them.

Although it is possible for us to fix this, a complex selector is required. Let us add the class of *teaser* to all the three columns making up our home page. The class will then be used as a selector within CSS. Here it is:

```
<section class="grid">
  <section class="teaser col-1-3">
    <a href="services.html">
      <h5>Services</h5>
      <h3>World-Class Serices</h3>
    </a>
    <p> We served different customers from
all over the world, and these are ready to
share their testimonies. </p>
  </section>

  ...
</section>
```

We can now apply some CSS to it. We will use the teaser class as the selector within our CSS since we are only targeting the elements that are within the *teaser* class. After that, we will need to apply styles to the elements belonging to the *teaser* class. After that, we will want to apply styles to hover elements that are hovered over, and that is why we will use the class selector together with the: hover pseudo-class. We will also use an h3 type selector so as to select all elements that belong to the <h3> element. This is shown below:

```
.teaser a:hover h3 {
    color: #a9b2b9;
}
```

Text Align

We should align our text on a web page so as to come up with a nice flow and rhythm for our web page. We can achieve this by use of the *text-align* property. This property can take 5 possible values namely *left, right, center, justify,* and *inherit.* Their meaning is self-explanatory as they align the text to either left, right, center, etc.

The CSS given below will align all the paragraphs to the left:

```
p {
    text-align: left;
}
```

However, do not confuse the *text-align* property with the *float* property. When you set the *text-align* property to right or left, the text will be moved to the right or left within an element. However, when you set the *float* property to right or left, the entire element will be moved. In some cases, we can get the desired result using the *text-align* property but in other cases, we have to use the *float* property.

Text Decoration

With the *text decoration* property, we can get a handful of ways to spruce up our text. It takes the values of either *none, underline, overline, line-through,* or *inherit.* The *text-decorator* property is used for various purposes, but it is mostly used for underlining links, which is the default style provided by web browsers.

Consider the following CSS that decorates any text that belongs to the class *note* by underlining it:

```
.note {
    text-decoration: underline;
}
```

You can apply multiple decoration styles to your text by specifying the styles and separating those using commas.

Text Indent

We can use the *text-indent* property when we need to indent the first line of text in an element, as it is the case in most publications. This property also takes values for common length text, including points, pixels, percentages, etc. When you use a text value, the text will be indented inwards, but when you use a negative value, the text will be indented outwards.

Consider the CSS given below:

```
p {
    text-indent: 30px;
}
```

The above indents the text for <p> elements inwards by 20 pixels.

Text Shadow

With the *text-shadow* property, we can add a shadow or many shadows to our text. The property accepts four values listed from left right. The first three values denote the lengths, while the last value denotes the color.

The first length value determines the horizontal offset of the shadow, the second value determines the vertical offset of the shadow while the third value determines the blur radius of the shadow. The fourth, which is the last value determines the color of the shadow, and this can be any value that can be used for the color property.

Consider the CSS given below:

```
p {
  text-shadow: 4px 6px 3px rgba(0, 0, 0,
  .3);
}
```

In the above example, we are casting the text 40% opaque black shadow 4 pixels to the right, 6 pixels down, and blurred 3 pixels of all the <p> element text.

When we use negative length values for horizontal and vertical offsets, the shadows will be moved towards the left and top.

We can chain multiple text shadows together using comma-separated values so as to add multiple shadows to the text. When we use multiple shadows, it becomes possible for us to place them below and above text, and have any variation that we may desire.

Text Transform

We use this property to change text inline without having to use an alternate typeface. The *text-transform* property accepts the values *none, capitalize, uppercase, lowercase,* and *inherit.*

When you use a value of *capitalizing,* the first letter of every word will be capitalized. A value of *uppercase* will capitalize every letter while a value of *lowercase* will write every letter in lowercase. If you use a value of *none,* the inherited values will be returned back to the original style of the text. Consider the example given below:

```
p {
  text-transform: lowercase;
}
```

The above CSS will make all <p> text to appear in lowercase.

Letter Spacing

We can use the *letter-spacing* property to adjust the amount of space that we add between letters on a page. If you use a positive value, the letters will be pushed farther apart from each other, while a negative value will move the letters closer to each other. A value of *none* for this property will return the space between the letters back to normal.

When we use a value of relative length for this property, a

correct spacing will be maintained between the letters since the *font-size* will also change. However, always ensure that you double-check your work.

Consider the CSS given below:

```
p {
  letter-spacing: -.5em;
}
```

With the above CSS, all letters that appear within the <p> element will be printed at 5 em closer to each other.

Word Spacing

This property helps us to adjust the space between words. The *word-spacing* property takes the same values as the *letter-spacing* property. Instead of adding space between letters, the *word-spacing* property applies to space between words.

Consider the CSS given below:

```
p {
  word-spacing: .20em;
}
```

With the above CSS, all words within the <p> element will be spaced at .20 em.

Putting all Together

We need to put all the above styles together and use them on our blog teaser. We have the following HTML:

```
<Html>
<header>
```

```
<link rel="stylesheet" href="mystyle.css">
</header>


<h2><a href="#">Web developer</a></h2>

<p class="byline">Posted by Alex</p>

<p> This example demonstrates how to use all
the CSS font properties <a
href="#">Continue&#8230;</a></p>

<Html>
```

Then here is the CSS for the file *mystyle.css:*

```
h2,
p {
  color: #654;
  font: 14px/22px "Helvetica Neue",
Helvetica, Arial, sans-serif;
}
a {
  color: #0287cc;
}
a:hover {
  color: #fc7b27;
}
h2 {
  font-size: 20px;
  font-weight: bold;
  margin-bottom: 8px;
  letter-spacing: -.02em;

}
h2 a {
  text-decoration: none;
  text-shadow: 2px 2px 1px rgba(0, 0, 0,
.2);
}
.byline {
```

```css
  color: #6759a6;
  font-family: Georgia, Times, "Times New
Roman", serif;
  font-style: italic;
  margin-bottom: 20px;
}
.intro {
  text-indent: 16px;
}
.intro a {
  font-size: 12px;
  font-weight: bold;
  text-decoration: underline;
  text-transform: uppercase;
}
```

These should return the following blog:

Web developer

Posted by Alex

This example demonstrates how to use all the CSS font properties Continue...

Practice

At this point, you should have the home page of the website, that is, My Website. You should have the following HTML code:

```html
<!DOCTYPE html>
<html lang="en">
<head>
<meta charset="utf-8">
<title>My Website</title>
<link rel="stylesheet" href="main.css">
</head>

<body>
<!-- Header -->
```

```html
<header class="container group">
<h1 class="logo">
<a href="index.html">My <br> Website</a>
</h1>
<h3 class="tagline">Welcome to My Website.
Enjoy our services</h3>
<nav class="nav primary-nav">
<a href="index.html">Home</a>
 <a href="about.html">About Us</a>
 <a href="services.html">Services</a>
 <a href="location.html">Location</a>
 <a href="contact.html">Contact Us</a>
 </nav>
 </header>

<!-- Hero -->
<section class="hero container">
<h2>World-Class Services</h2>
 <p>Enjoy our Services</p>
<a class="btn btn-alt"
href="contact.html">Contact us Now</a>
</section>


<!-- Teasers -->
<section class="grid">

<!-- About Us -->
<section class="teaser col-1-3">
<a href="about.html">
<h5>Service</h5>
<h3>World-Class Services</h3>
</a>
<p>We served different customers from all
over the world, and these are ready to share
their testimonies.</p>
</section>

<!--    Location    -->
<section class="teaser col-1-3">
```

```
<a href="location.html">
<h5>Location</h5>
  <h3>You can find us at</h3>
</a>
<p>We are available throughout the week.
</p>
</section>


<!--      Contact      -->
<section class="teaser col-1-3">
 <a href="contact.html">
<h5>Contact Us</h5>
<h3>Call us on ...</h3>
</a>
<p>You can contact us any day of the week
between 8:00am and 9:00pm</p>
 </section>
</section>


<!-- Footer -->
<footer class="primary-footer container
group">
<small>&copy; My Website</small>

 <nav class="nav">
<a href="index.html">Home</a>
   <a href="about.html">About Us</a>
    <a href="services.html">Services</a>
    <a href="location.html">Location</a>
    <a href="contact.html">Contact Us</a>
 </nav>
</footer>
</body>
</html>
```

The corresponding CSS code for the file
main.css should now be as follows:

```
/*
  Grid
*/
*,
```

```css
*:before,
*:after {
  -webkit-box-sizing: border-box;
     -moz-box-sizing: border-box;
          box-sizing: border-box;
}

.col-1-3 {
  width: 33.33%;
}
.col-2-3 {
  width: 66.66%;
}
col-1-3,
.col-2-3 {
  display: inline-block;
  vertical-align: top;
}

.grid,
.col-1-3,
.col-2-3 {
  padding-left: 15px;
  padding-right: 15px;
}

.container,
.grid {
  margin: 0 auto;
  width: 960px;
}
.container {
  padding-left: 30px;
  padding-right: 30px;
}

.container {
  margin: 0 auto;
  padding-left: 30px;
  padding-right: 30px;
```

```css
  width: 960px;
}

h1, h3, h4, h5, p {
  margin-bottom: 22px;
}

.btn {
  border-radius: 5px;
  display: inline-block;
  margin: 0;
}

.btn-alt {
  border: 1px solid #dfe2e5;
  padding: 10px 30px;
}

.hero {
  line-height: 44px;
  padding: 22px 80px 66px 80px;
}
.hero h2 {
  font-size: 36px;
}
.hero p {
  font-size: 24px;
}

body {
  color: #768;
  font: 300 18px/20px "Open Sans",
"Helvetica Neue", Helvetica, Arial, sans-
serif;
}

h1, h2, h3, h4 {
  color: #728882;
}
```

```css
h1 {
  font-size: 34px;
  line-height: 42px;
}
h2 {
  font-size: 22px;
  line-height: 42px;
}
h3 {
  font-size: 20px;
}
h4 {
  font-size: 17px;
}


h5 {
  color: #a8c2b7;
  font-size: 14px;
  font-weight: 400;
}

strong {
  font-weight: 400;
}
cite, em {
  font-style: italic;
}


a:hover {
  color: #a9b2b9;
}
a {
  color: #648880;
}

.logo {
  border-top: 4px solid #648880;
```

```
  float: left;
  font-size: 48px;
  line-height: 44px;
  padding: 40px 0 22px 0;
}



.tagline {
  margin: 66px 0 22px 0;
}


.primary-nav {
  font-size: 14px;
  font-weight: 400;
}



.primary-footer {
  color: #758890;
  font-size: 14px;
  padding-bottom: 44px;
  padding-top: 44px;
}
.primary-footer small {
  float: left;
  font-weight: 400;
}
```

8-Creating Forms

Forms are very important when it comes to web development. They help us to collect data from users and they come with nearly every form of control that is essential for such tasks. By use of a number of controls, forms can ask for information from users.

The form controls can be created using HTML. To style the form, we can use CSS. Let us discuss this:

Initializing Forms

Anytime you need to add a form to a web page, use the <form> element. This will determine where you will have the form controls on the web page. This element will also wrap everything that is added to the form. The initialization of a form can be done as follows:

```
<form action="/login" method="post">
    . . .
</form>
```

There are various attributes that we can apply to the <form>

element, but the most popular ones are the *action* and *method* attributes. The action attribute helps us specify the URL to which information added to the form will be sent for processing. The *method* attribute denotes the HTTP method that web browsers will use so as to submit the form data.

Text Fields

A text field I a form element that can be used for gathering data from users. To create a text field, use the <input> element. The <input> element uses the *type* attribute to specify the type of data that is to be captured within that text field. The common value for the *type* attribute is *text*.

Other than the *type* attribute, it is always good for you to assign a value to the *name* attribute when create a text field. This value will be used as the unique identifier for the control. The following HTML code demonstrates how to create a text field:

```
<Html>
<header>
</header>
<body>
<input type="text" name="username">
</body>
</Html>
```

The code should return the following:

That above is a text field. It will expect you to enter an input data of type text. The text field has been given the name *username*.

Other than *text,* there are various other values that we can use for the *type* attribute of <input> element depending on the kind of data that you need to capture. Most of these have been introduced in HTML5. They include the following:

- Color
- Datetime
- date
- email
- month
- range
- number
- search
- tel
- url
- time
- week

The following HTML code demonstrates how to use or create some of the above input elements:

```
<Html>
<header>
</header>
<body>
<input type="date" name="enrollmentdate">
<br /> <br />
<input type="time" name="class-time"> <br />
<br />
<input type="email" name="email-address">
<br /> <br />
<input type="url" name="profile"> <br /> <br
/>
<input type="number" name="fee"> <br /> <br
/>
```

```
<input type="tel" name="phone-number"> <br
/> <br />
</body>
</Html>
```

The code should return the following input elements:

```
mm/dd/yyyy
```

```
-- : -- --
```

```

```

```

```

```

```

```

```

Textarea

The textarea is another element that we use to capture text-based data. It is created by use of the <textarea> element. The difference between a text field and a textarea is that a textarea can accept a larger text that spans multiple lines.

The <textarea> has both opening and closing tags and it can enclose a plain text within the tags. Since the textarea can only accept one type of value, it doesn't take the *type* attribute but it takes the *name* attribute. Consider the example given below:

```
<Html>
<header>
</header>
<body>
```

```
<textarea name="comment">Your comment goes
here ...</textarea>
</body>
</Html>
```

This returns the following output:

```
Your comment goes
here ...
```

There are two attributes that we can use to size the <textarea> element. First, we have the *cols* that determine the width in terms of the average character width. Secondly, we have the *rows* which determine the height in terms of number of visible lines of text. However, the size of a textarea is mostly set using the *width* and *height* properties within CSS.

Radio Buttons

In HTML, there are elements that can help us enter data when we have multiple choices. A good example of such an element is the radio button. Radio buttons allow a user to make a quick decision from a list of options.

To create a radio button, we use the <input> element and a *type* attribute value of *radio*. Each element of the radio button should have a similar *name* attribute for buttons belonging to the same group to be bale able to correspond to each other.

When dealing with text-based inputs, the value of an input depends on what a user types in, but for the case of radio buttons, the user is provided with multiple choices to choose from. This means that we are required to define the value. When we use the *value* attribute, it becomes possible for us to set the specific value for every <input> element. If we need to have one of the radio buttons pre-selected, we can use the Boolean attributed *checked*. Consider the example given below:

```
<Html>
<header>
</header>
<body>
<input type="radio" name="gender"
value="Male" checked> Male
<input type="radio" name="gender"
value="Female"> Female
</body>
</Html>
```

The code should return the following:

⦿ Male ◯ Female

Check Boxes

Checkboxes are similar to the radio buttons. They all use similar attributes and patterns, with the difference being the checkbox as their type attribute value. The main difference between the two is that a checkbox allows a user to select multiple values at once and tie them to a single control name, but with radio buttons, one can only choose one value.

A checkbox is also created using the <input> element but the value of the *type* attribute should be set to *checkbox*. If we need to have one of the options checked by default, we can use the

Boolean attribute *checked*. Consider the example given below:

```
<Html>
<header>
</header>
<body>
<input type="checkbox" name="gender"
value="Male" checked> Male
<input type="checkbox" name="gender"
value="Female"> Female
</body>
</Html>
```

The code will return the following:

☑ Male ☐ Female

Drop-Down Lists

Drop-down lists are a good way of provided users with a long list of options more practically. When we use multiple radio buttons, it may be unappealing to users especially to users using mobile devices. Drop-down lists form the best option when we have a long list of choices to choose from.

When creating a drop-down list, we use the <select> and <option> elements. The <select> element will wrap all the menu options, and the menus are marked using the <option> element.

The *name* attribute will reside in the <select> element, while the *value* attribute resides in the <option> elements that have been nested within the <select> element. Every <option> element should wrap the text of an option within the list, and this is visible to the users.

In the radio button and checkboxes, we used the *checked* Boolean attribute to specify the default selected option. For the drop-down list, we can use the *selected* attribute to set the default selected element. Consider the example given below:

```
<Html>
<header>
</header>
<body>
<select name="gender">
  <option value="Male"
selected>Male</option>
  <option value="Female">Female</option>
</select>
</body>
</Html>
```

The code should generate the following:

When you click the drop-down button, you will be able to see all the options that are available.

With a drop-down list, it is possible for a user to choose more than one items at a time. To achieve this, we use a Boolean attribute named *multiple*. When you use the *selected* attribute within the <option> element, you will get many preselected items.

You can modify the size of the <select> element within CSS, especially its size. If a user needs to choose multiple options, they have to hold down the Shift key while making the selection. Here is how to create such a <select> element:

```
<Html>
<header>
</header>
<body>
<select name="gender" multiple>
  <option value="Male"
selected>Male</option>
  <option value="Female">Female</option>
</select>
</body>
</Html>
```

This should return the following select element:

To choose both items, make sure that you hold down the shift key when making the selection.

Now that you know the various elements that can be used to capture data from the user, you SHOULD know the various buttons that we can use to submit the data.

Submit Input

The user clicks the submit button after filling a form so as to submit the form data for processing. To create this button, we use the <input> element and use a value of *submit* for the *type* attribute. The text to be shown on the button is added using the *value* attribute. The following example demonstrates how to create such a button:

```
<Html>
<header>
</header>
<body>
<input type="submit" name="submit"
value="Send">
</body>
</Html>
```

The code should return the following button:

Send

Submit Button

This is a self-contained button that cannot be used for wrapping any other content. If there is a desire to have more control over the input, you can use the <button> element.

The <button> element is the same as the <input> element, taking a value of *submitting* for the *type* attribute. However, it takes both opening and closing tags, which we may use to wrap other elements. The default setting is that the <button> elements acts as if it has a default value of *submitting* for the *type* attribute. The <button> element allows you to omit the *value* attribute if your wish to.

Instead of using the *value* attribute to specify the text that will appear on the button, the text added within the opening and closing <button> tags will be added to the button. Here is the example:

```
<Html>
```

```
<header>
</header>
<body>
<button name="submit">
  <strong>Submit</strong> data
</button>
</body>
</Html>
```

The code will return the following button:

Submit data

Other than what we have discussed above, the <input>
element has several other uses. Let us discuss them:

Hidden Input

With hidden input, we can pass data to the server without
having to show it to the users. Hidden inputs are good for tracing
codes, keys and other information that is not important to the user
but it is good when it comes to processing the form. Although the
information is not displayed on the page, one can view it by
viewing the source code for the page. That is why this should not
be used for sensitive or secure information.

When you need to create a hidden input, use the *hidden* value
for the *type* attribute. You should also include the correct value for
the *name* and *value* attributes.

Consider the example given below:

```
<Html>
<header>
</header>
<body>
```

```
<input type="hidden" name="code-track"
value="xyz">
</body>
</Html>
```

The code will not return a button.

File Input

Sometimes, you may need users to attach a file to a form in the same way that you attach a file to an email. This is possible by using the value of *file* for the *type* attribute. The following example demonstrates this:

```
<Html>
<header>
</header>
<body>
<input type="file" name="file">
</body>
</Html>
```

This will return the following:

Choose File | No file chosen

When you click the Choose File button, the file dialog will be opened allowing you to browse through your computer to choose a file for uploading.

However, it is hard to style the <input> of type *file* in CSS. Each web browser comes with its own style for the file input type and we are not much allowed to override these styles.

Now you know how to capture data of different types from the users. However, this is just half of the work. You should know how to organize them so that you may have nice-looking forms. You need a way of guiding the users on the type of information that they should provide. This can be done using fieldsets, labels, and legends. Let us discuss these:

Label

Labels help in providing headings or captions for the form controls, making it easy for users to know the kind of information they should supply in various form controls. To create a label, use the <label> element and add the text that will be used for describing the control.

You can add the *for* attribute to the <label> element. The value of this attribute should match the value of *id* attribute of the control in question. This has the effect of tying the two elements together, and users will be able to click the <label> element and get a focus on the right form of control.

The following example demonstrates this:

```
<Html>
<header>
</header>
<body>
<label for="username">Username</label>
<input type="text" name="username"
id="username">
</body>
</Html>
```

The code generates the following controls:

Username

The value for the *for* attribute in <label> element is similar to the value for *id* attribute in the <input> element. To see this work, click the *Username* label on the form. You will see a cursor inside the correct form control waiting for your input:

Username |

We can also use the <label> element to wrap form controls together. Examples of such controls include radio buttons and checkboxes. In such a case, we can omit the *for* and *id* attributes. The following example demonstrates this:

```
<Html>
<header>
</header>
<body>
<label>
<input type="radio" name="gender"
value="Male" checked> Male
</label>
<label>
  <input type="radio" name="gender"
value="Female"> Female
</label>
</body>
</Html>
```

The code will return the following:

⦿ Male ◯ Female

As you have noticed, we have wrapped each <input> element for creating each radio button within the <label> element.

Fieldsets

The purpose of fieldsets is to group labels and form controls into more organized sections. Just like structural elements such as <section>, the <fieldset> wraps related elements together and it is a bloc-level element. By default, <fieldset> element comes with a border line that can be modified via CSS. Consider the example given below:

```
<Html>
<header>
</header>
<body>
<fieldset>
  <label>
    Username
    <input type="text" name="username"> <br
/> <br />
  </label>
  <label>
    Password
    <input type="text" name="password">
  </label>
</fieldset>
</body>
</Html>
```

The form controls will be surrounded by a borderline, which is generated by the fieldset.

| Username | |
| Password | |

Legend

The purpose of a <legend> element is to provide a heading or caption for <fieldset> element. The <legend> should come immediately after the <fieldset> element. Consider the example given below:

```
<Html>
<header>
</header>
<body>
<fieldset>
  <legend>Login</legend>
  <label>
    Username
    <input type="text" name="username"> <br
/> <br />
  </label>
  <label>
    Password
    <input type="text" name="password">
  </label>
</fieldset>
</body>
</Html>
```

The code should return the following output:

There are also attributes that we can use in forms. These attributes serve a number of different purposes, including addition of validation and disabling the controls. Let us discuss some of these attributes:

Disabled

This is a Boolean attribute that turns a control on or off for interaction with users or receiving of input. If an element is disabled, it will not send data to the server for processing.

If we apply the *disabled* attribute to the <fieldset> element, all the elements added to this will be disabled. The following example demonstrates this:

```
<Html>
<header>
</header>
<body>
<label>
Username
<input type="text" name="username" disabled>
</label>
</body>
</Html>
```

The code should generate the following output:

Username

As you can see, we can type nothing into the input field. This is because it has been marked as *disabled.*

Placeholder

This attribute was introduced in HTML5 and it helps in providing a hint in a <input> or <textarea> element and it will disappear when the control is clicked or when you focus on it. It helps in providing users with additional information and guide them on how to fill the form. A good example is when you need users to fill in their email addresses. You can use a placeholder to give them the format that you expect. For example:

```
<Html>
<header>
</header>
<body>
<label>
  Email Address
  <input type="email" name="emailaddress"
placeholder="name@domain.com">
</label>
</body>
</Html>
```

The code returns the following:

Email Address `name@domain.com`

The *name@domain.com* was added to the control using the *placeholder* attribute.

R e q u i r e d

This attribute was introduced in HTML5 and it states that a form of control must have value prior to the submission of the form data to the server for processing. If the form control does not have a value, an error message will be displayed asking the user to fill the form control with a value. Such error messages are controlled by the default styles of the web browser but we cannot style them using CSS. For the invalid form controls and elements, you can style them using the: *required* and: *optional* CSS pseudo-classes.

The validation is also specific to controls. A good example is when you have an <input> element with a value of *email* for the *type* attribute. This will require that the value for the email address be entered and at the same time, it must be a valid email address. Consider the example given below:

```
<Html>
<header>
</header>
<body>
<label>
  Email Address
  <input type="email" name="email-address"
required>
</label>
</body>
</Html>
```

The code should generate the following:

Email Address [   ]

Practice

In this practice exercise, we will create a login form. This form will take in various attributes that will help in demonstrating the various elements that we have discussed above. We will also use CSS to style these elements.

First, create the file *form.html*. Add the following code to the file:

```
<Html>
<header>
```

```html
<meta charset="utf-8">

<link rel="stylesheet" href="mystyle.css">

</header>
<body>
<form>
  <fieldset class="user-account">
    <label>
      Username
      <input type="text" name="username">
    </label>
    <label>
      Password
      <input type="password"
name="password">
    </label>
  </fieldset>
  <fieldset class="account-action">
    <input class="btn" type="submit"
name="submit" value="Login">
    <label>
      <input type="checkbox"
name="remember"> Remember Me?
    </label>
  </fieldset>
</form>
</body>
</Html>
```

Create the CSS file, mystyle.css and add the following code to it:

```css
*,
*:before,
*:after {
  box-sizing: border-box;
}
form {
  border: 2px solid #c7c7cc;
  border-radius: 5px;
```

```css
  font: 14px/1.4 "Helvetica Neue",
Helvetica, Arial, sans-serif;
  overflow: hidden;
  width: 240px;
}
fieldset {
  border: 0;
  margin: 0;
  padding: 0;
}
input {
  border-radius: 5px;
  font: 14px/1.4 "Helvetica Neue",
Helvetica, Arial, sans-serif;
  margin: 0;
}
.account-info {
  padding: 20px 20px 0 20px;
}
.account-info label {
  color: #495862;
  display: block;
  font-weight: bold;
  margin-bottom: 20px;
}
.account-info input {
  background: #cff;
  border: 1px solid #c6c7cc;
   box-shadow: inset 0 1px 1px rgba(0, 0, 0,
.1);
  color: #746466;
  padding: 6px;
  margin-top: 6px;
  width: 100%;
}
.account-action {
  background: #f0f0f2;
  border-top: 1px solid #c6c7cc;
  padding: 20px;
}
```

```css
.account-action .btn {
  background: linear-gradient(#49708f,
#293f50);
  border: 0;
  color: #cff;
  cursor: pointer;
  font-weight: bold;
  float: left;
  padding: 8px 16px;
}
.account-action label {
  color: #7c7c80;
  font-size: 12px;
  float: left;
  margin: 10px 0 0 20px;
}
```

The codes should result into the following form:

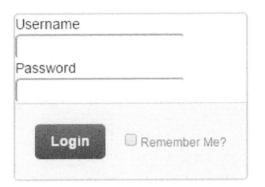

9-Tables

Tables are normally used for the purpose of displaying data to the users. In some cases, tables are used for dividing the web pages but avoid this as they are less flexible compared to the *divs*.

Table are created using the <table> element. It should be the first element in a table and it states that the other markups will be inside a table. Tables are structured using rows and columns. However, columns have no tags unlike rows. Each row is created using the <tr> tag for table row, while each cell is created using the <td> data which means table data. You must define the structure of your table before beginning to create it as this will make it easy for you to create it. The following is an example of a simple table:

```
<Html>
<header>
</header>
<body>
<table border="1" width="100%">
<tr>
<td>Cell 1 at Row 1</td>
<td>Cell 2 at Row 1</td>
<td>Cell 3 at Row 2</td>
</tr>
<tr>
<td>Cell 1 at Row 2</td>
<td>Cell 2 at Row 2</td>
<td>Cell 3 at Row 2</td>
</tr>
<tr>
<td>Cell 1 at Row 3</td>
<td>Cell 2 at Row 3</td>
<td>Cell 3 at Row 3</td>
</tr>
```

```
<tr>
<td>Cell 1 at Row 4</td>
<td>Cell 2 at Row 4</td>
<td>Cell 3 at Row 4</td>
</tr>
</table>

</body>
</Html>
```

The code will generate the following output:

Cell 1 at Row 1	Cell 2 at Row 1	Cell 3 at Row 2
Cell 1 at Row 2	Cell 2 at Row 2	Cell 3 at Row 2
Cell 1 at Row 3	Cell 2 at Row 3	Cell 3 at Row 3
Cell 1 at Row 4	Cell 2 at Row 4	Cell 3 at Row 4

As you have seen in the above table, each <td> tag is inside a <tr> tag. All the <td> tags inside one <tr> tag will be added to the same row.

Colspan and Rowspan

HTML markup has been designed in such a way that you can add a different number of cells into a row. In some rows, you can have four cells, three cells in others, etc. For you to achieve this, you must use the colspan and rowspan attributes. These attributes normally take a whole number as the value.

Let us use our previous example but make the first row to have two cells rather than three. We will also be merging and second cell of rows three and four:

```
<Html>
<header>
</header>
<body>
<table border="1" width="100%">
<tr>
<td colspan="2">Cell 1 at Row 1</td>
<td>Cell 2 at Row 1</td>
</tr>
<tr>
<td>Cell 1 at Row 2</td>
<td>Cell 2 at Row 2</td>
<td>Cell 3 at Row 2</td>
</tr>
<tr>
<td>Cell 1 at Row 3</td>
<td>Cell 2 at Row 3</td>
<td>Cell 3 at Row 3</td>
</tr>
<tr>
<td>Cell 1 at Row 4</td>
<td>Cell 2 at Row 4</td>
<td>Cell 3 at Row 4</td>
</tr>
</table>

</body>
</Html>
```

This gives the following table:

Cell 1 at Row 1		Cell 2 at Row 1
Cell 1 at Row 2	Cell 2 at Row 2	Cell 3 at Row 2
Cell 1 at Row 3	Cell 2 at Row 3	Cell 3 at Row 3
Cell 1 at Row 4	Cell 2 at Row 4	Cell 3 at Row 4

In the first row, we have used the colspan attribute so that the first cell can occupy two columns. In the third row, we have used the rowspan attribute so that the second row spans two rows. The cell that is occupied after spanning the columns or the rows has been removed.

Changing Column Width

You can use percentages to alter the width of your table columns. The width of all columns in a row should add up to 100%. This can be done using the *col* attribute as shown below:

```
<Html>
<header>
</header>
<body>
<table border="1" width="100%">
<col style="width:40%">
<col style="width:30%">
<col style="width:30%">
<thead>
<tr>
<th>Name</th>
<th>Subject</th>
<th>Marks</th>
</tr>
</thead>
<tbody>
<tr>
<th>John</th>
<td>Maths</td>
<td>55</td>
</tr>
<tr>
<th>Nicholas</th>
```

```
<td>Physics</td>
<td>77</td>
</tr>
<tr>
<th>Lilian</th>
<td>Biology</td>
<td>58</td>
</tr>
</tbody>
</table>
</body>
</Html>
```

The code should return the following table:

Name	Subject	Marks
John	Maths	55
Nicholas	Physics	77
Lilian	Biology	58

That is how you can control the width of your table

Conclusion

This marks the end of this book. HTML is a web programming language that helps us to create the elements and content that we need to add to a web page. With HTML, we can create and add the elements to the web page. However, this will not give the web pages the structure that we need. To add styles and structure to the web pages, we need CSS. It is the language that we use to add text styles such as font, italics, bold, etc. With CSS, we can place each element on a web page in the right position. To write and run HTML and CSS codes, you only need a basic text editor such as Notepad in Windows and a web browser.

HTML5 is the latest version of HTML while CSS3 is the latest version of CSS. The two have introduced new features that you can take advantage of to develop a good-looking website. For instance, with HTML5, you don't need JavaScript for validation of your forms. With CSS3, you can create responsive web pages that scale well based on the size of the screen of the device under use.

ABOUT THE AUTHOR

Daniel Bell was born in the Bronx, New York. When he was nine, he moved with his father Guy Bell to Nice in France. He received his Ph.D. degree in computer science from the University of Nice (France) in 2012. Daniel is conducting research in data management, with an emphasis on topics related to Big Data and data sharing, such as probabilistic data, data pricing, parallel data processing, data security. He spends his free time writing books on computer programming and data science, to help the absolute beginners in computer programming to code easily. He lives in Chatillon, near Paris.

Acknowledgments

Foremost, I would like to express my sincere gratitude to my family, my wife Genevieve and my son Adan for the continuous support in my everyday life, for their patience, motivation, enthusiasm. Besides my family, I would like to thank my friends and colleagues: Prof. Jule Villepreux, Hugo D. and Dr. James Rivera, for their encouragement, insightful comments, and hard questions. I thank my fellow labmates: Gang Yu, Ting Fan, Djibrilla Diallo, Juan Sanchez, for the stimulating discussions, for the sleepless nights we were working together before deadlines, and for all the fun we have had. Last but not least, I would like to thank my parents Guy Bell and Ezra Bell, for giving birth to me at the first place and supporting me spiritually throughout my life

www.guzzlermedia.com

Printed in Great Britain
by Amazon

42736557R00088